The Expedition: Do You

A 12 step based approach to self-love

By
Amber Haehnel

Disclaimer

The authors have made every effort to ensure that the information in this book was correct at press time. The authors do not assume and hereby disclaim any liability to any party for any loss, damage, or disruption caused by errors or omissions, whether such errors or omissions result from accident, or any other cause.

Due to the variability of materials and skills, the authors assume no responsibility for any personal injury, property damage, or other loss of any sort suffered from any actions taken based on or inspired by information or advice herein. Make sure you completely understand any procedure before beginning work. If ever uncertain, consult a professional.

Copyright © 2019 Amber Haehnel

All rights reserved. This book or any portion thereof may not be reproduced or used in any manner whatsoever without the express written permission of the publisher except for the use of brief quotations in a book review.

Printed in the United States of America

ISBN: 9781796526035

For all the girls who are still searching for their true selves.

For all the girls who need something more out of life.

For all the girls who are trying to figure out their worth.

I love you.

I am with you.

We are in this together.

Acknowledgements

What an amazing adventure this has been and will be.

First, I will take a moment to thank my husband, Chad. What a roller coaster we have been riding, with only the best of outcomes. Without you, this would not have happened, my self-discovery may have happened over time, but our struggles together, though incredibly difficult, allowed me the space to become who I was meant to be and do what I was created to do. You have paved the way for turning something I thought would destroy us into the very thing that has grown our marriage and our lives, which has also walked me right into the path of writing and helping others. The discovery of my own self-love and development of a plan to attain it could not have been done without each and every step we took to become better people, and better partners. I am so proud of the person you are and who we are becoming together. Thank you for your patience, teaching me patience and empathy. For you, I am forever grateful.

Magical Mentorship class of 2018 – You are my solidarity, my rocks, and my constants in life. Without your never ending encouragement and belief, this would not be a reality for me. I cannot express my gratitude for each and every one of you on this ride with me. We are forever #MM18 and I cherish you for bringing me to life.

To all Featured Females – wow. I am blown away by each of you, your honesty and willingness to share. I was amazed that each of you said yes to sharing your voice with me and the world, I know it was not necessarily easy. I love you dearly, and I'm so humbled and grateful you decided to do this with me.

Kendall, Teresa, Keeli – You are my soul sisters and my world would not be nearly as honest, colorful and exciting without each of you. Thank you for putting up with me during this process. I love you.

Dr. Sarah Schonian – I am so grateful for writing sessions, coffee, talking, brainstorming and sharing with one another. Thank you for listening, and most of all, encouraging me to write.

Fearless Kind – I am beyond grateful for this organization that taught me how to be myself again, how to get back to who I am and learn to focus inward to fix any situation.

Recover Everything Podcast – Thank you for having me as a guest, allowing me to share my story, struggles and promote this book. You all are doing amazing work, and I am excited to see where the future takes you.

My family – Thank you for your never-ending support, even with all my crazy ideas. I love you.

To each and every person who was excited about this – who took the time to send me an encouraging message, to ask when I will be launching or pre-selling, who said they couldn't wait for me to publish. You are the reason I did all of this, and I am eternally grateful for your support and excitement.

And finally, to Heidi – you never stopped encouraging me to be exactly what I wanted and go after anything no matter how crazy it seemed. You have a view that I could do anything in the world and made me believe that. You are forever a light in my life. Without you, this book would probably be sitting on my computer unseen.

Table of Contents

Introduction..13
   My story...15
   What qualifies me for such a task? 18
   This is ME..19

Chapter 1: 27
   It takes a tribe..29
   So, here you are 33
   Here are some things you need to know:................33
   Trust the process 34
   Reflection:...38
   This is ME..39

Chapter 2: 45
   You get to be the change you wish to see. 47
   Letting go...48
   The Big Moment..50
   Excuses 52
   Reflections: 55
   This is ME..56

Chapter 3: 61
   Well, you are here. You made it this far................63

A Trusted Confidant. 63
　Pride 66
　Self esteem 67
　Relationships 68
　Ambitions 69
　Reflections: 70
　Questions to determine the right person for this job: 70
　Some tips on this: 71
　This is ME 72

Chapter 4: 79
　Are you ready for the fun? 81
　Insecurities 85
　Self-Doubts 87
　Questions to spark the mind: 90
　This is ME 93

Chapter 5: 99
　Hold up… 102
　Taking Control… 105
　Some questions to reflect on: 106
　Ideas on how to talk to your person: 107

Chapter 6: 109
　Meditation 111
　Mindfulness 113
　Making a Change 114
　Reflection questions: 120
　This is ME 121

This is ME 126

Chapter 7: **131**
    Find a ritual 136
    Post it up 137
    Meditation and Mindfulness 137
    Write a letter to yourself 138
    Talk it out 138
    Take Massive Action 139
    Reflection questions: 140
    This is ME 141

Chapter 8: **145**
    Apologize 149
    Close Encounters of the Doubting Kind 151
    Same Situations 152
    Some questions to think on: 154
    This is ME 155

Chapter 9: **159**
    Greatest Good 161
    Things 162
    Here are some questions for this process: 162
    People 165
    Habits 167
    Here are some questions to ask yourself in this step: 171
    This is ME 172
    This is ME 178

Chapter 10: **185**

    Be aware 187

    Fuck ups 189

    Some questions to reflect on: 193

    This is ME 194

    This is ME 198

Chapter 11: **205**

    Taking back your power 207

    Drop the victim mentality 209

    Take ownership of your life 211

    Forgive Others 213

    Policies 215

    This is ME 218

    This is ME 222

Chapter 12: **229**

    Staying connected 232

    Helping others 234

    Questions to reflect on: 235

    This is ME 236

Closing **252**

Introduction

Expedition: a journey or voyage undertaken by a group of people with a particular purpose.

When one person helps another, we strengthen our bond and sense of community with one another. I am a firm believer, who believes that in order to start an expedition – any expedition in life – you need a tribe of people there to support and hold you accountable along the way.

I started this as a journey set out by myself, and I kept coming back to the word expedition. It stuck with me, and I knew I needed more people to come along with me, to keep me accountable as I went, and to work on themselves alongside me.

Thus, the "Do You Expedition" was born.

So, here we go.

Let's start with an understanding of love itself.

Love is the most powerful thing on the planet. It overcomes hate, drives out fear, grows the heart, mends the terrible and brings light.

We are able to give love and receive love; unfortunately, most of us cannot give and receive love from our most important relationship – ourselves.

This is the foundation of love, where it grows, resides, and starts. We cannot truly give and receive love to others fully, until we start loving ourselves.

This relationship – the one you have with you – is the most important and longest of your life. You know yourself better than anyone else does; so, why is it so difficult to truly love ourselves, for exactly who we are in this moment?

It is my belief we are constantly told not to, and we do not take full responsibility for our owns lives.

I hear it all the time, when I lose weight, when I find the love of my life, when I get rid of this acne (guilty), when I find a good job, when I move into a new apartment, etc., then I will work on myself.

Why do we wait? When the foundation of everything we want and need in life resides right here in ourselves. This journey gets to be started, with a firm foundation, and no excuses; so that we can be fully loved and present in other areas of our lives.

Without true self-love, nothing more will be accomplished.

My story

It all started with this story. The story of my marriage. Being newly married should be everything all the people tell you it is, full of love, sex and inseparable to the point of annoyance to everyone you know.

Unfortunately, this was not our case. We both knew there was a problem, far before we ever brought it up. He knew, but refused to admit it to himself or anyone else. I knew, and out of fear of losing something so important to me, I refused to admit it to myself. I probably told everyone else (I trusted) about it, though. It was me who refused to actually believe it.

But there it was, alcohol addiction. He feeling attached constantly, me feeling unloved the majority of the time, and we fighting non-stop for the majority of the first year of our marriage.

The addiction and all the issues that came with it are for another time. The fact I felt unloved is what this is about. I felt unloved because I refused to believe I deserved love, which may be the reason I denied the problem for so long. I was angry because I refused to forgive myself for every mistake and issue I had ever made in my life. I was miserable because I was completely unhappy with myself. Yes, the addiction was an issue that brought all of this to the surface, but my unhappiness and misery were separate issues, which took me an exuberant amount of time to come to terms with.

The truth is that I was unhappy in my marriage because I was unhappy with myself.

I said all the things we all say, when I…that phrase was on repeat in my head like Call Me. Maybe it rang in all our heads for most of the year 2012. When I lose weight, when I get that job, when I save more money, when I can go on vacation, when I can complete my paper, when I finish this project…. after all those things, then I will be happy. I was reflecting my unhappiness on every single thing in my life; in order to avoid actually dealing with the fact - myself.

It wasn't my job, it wasn't the amount of money in my bank account, it wasn't my husband, or the size of my pants, or even the friends I kept. It was all on me.

With that realization, I made it clear to myself this was my responsibility, and I took that as my direct obligation. To figure out how to be happy, right this moment, with me, exactly as I am right now. Without doing that, I knew nothing would change.

Que in the twelve steps. I thought this was such a crock, and mocked it for the first few months in my life. I was proud of my husband for trying something new, to make himself a better human, but I didn't need something like that. The twelve steps were something in the movies, something sick people needed, and most definitely not something I needed to introduce.

At a time, I was resentful, and pushed them away; however, I knew in order to support my husband, I needed to do some sort of researches, but definitely not investing a lot of time, I had already invested most of my time in him, and was already partially resentful for that.

And then, the rainbow broke through the clouds, and I actually read the twelve exact steps that would change my life. No, this is not going to be a book about alcoholism, that is for another day. Everything happens on purpose, right? Not for a reason, terribly cliché, but for a purpose. I believed it anyway. And my resistance was to prevent me from ignoring these steps; so, by the time I introduced them to myself, I was ready.

I jumped in head first. The amount of research I put in could have finished a dissertation…now, that's an idea. Sidebar.

I put so much energy into the twelve steps and how they could be adjusted to those of us who needed something, a program of some sorts to help us in our day to day lives. They could be adjusted to be of the utmost assistance in helping us discover just how much we love ourselves, and how much we need to wake up to our own lives.

And thus, the "Do You Expedition" was born. And it has transformed my life completely. So, I pass on this information in the hope that it will transform yours as well.

What qualifies me for such a task?

Well, not only everything I mentioned in my story, but I am also an anthropologist; which means I have studied relentlessly the evolution of humans, how we process information, how we age, how we act in different cultures, what culture is, how we interact with one another…. you get the point? I have immense knowledge of the human creature itself.

I have tested out my steps to the fullest, I mean it when I say I took this as my direct obligation. Every step I dug in to thoroughly and practiced over and over, and still do to this day. I have put in to practice what I tell others to put in to practice, and I will never expect someone to do something I, myself, am not willing to do or have not done already. I am in the trenches with you, and will stay there with you, until we can move on together.

With all this said, I say unto you, my dear friend, you have the power to change your life at any moment you decide to do so. You are powerful and courageous and strong. You and only you have to wake up to your full potential and come alive in your life. It starts with love, and until you can break down all else and really love who you truly are at your core, you will not be living a fulfilling life. And darling, you deserve to live the most fulfilling life you could ever imagine.

Featured Female – Amber Haehnel

This is ME

I knew what it looks like when writing a book on self-love; examples would for sure be needed. So, I decided to have some featured females lined up the following chapters.

We all came from different walks of life, different situations, and different backgrounds; so, it just makes sense to list out different women's views on what self-love really means to them, and how it can apply to you. You may not relate directly to me and what I have been through, which is why I want to provide as many examples as possible, so that you can find someone you can truly relate to.

I will introduce myself first; so you know me from the start.

Who are you as a human being?

I am Amber. I grew up as a lower-middle-class military. There definitely needs to be a separate category for military families when it comes to disturbing class assignments, and if you grew up as military, I know you feel me on this one. Usually, I would not mention this, but growing up this way has played a major role in who I am as a human being. We were structured to a T, but moved often, which lead to a somewhat lonely existence, saying hello and goodbye so often – I honestly don't know how my mom did it. However, my parents always made us feel loved and provided for. No struggle nor sad stories, as we had an excellent childhood.

However, I was taught to always look forward, which was fantastic and paved a path for the future, but we never celebrated where we were. There was always something more coming in the future, and once we are there, something else would become the main focus. This led to low self-esteem (a feeling of not good enough), or like I could never celebrate any actual achievements, just keep looking forward to the next thing. The striving for more became never being the moment and enjoying it for what it was, which I have carried with myself and did not realize until recently. All this time, I could have been celebrating milestones and enjoying the moment and never did. As I sat writing this, I am already thinking of the next thing, instead of celebrating the fact that this is the last step before I release this freaking book. Luckily, it is never too late. Let's take a break for a thirty-second dance party.

I am the wife of an alcoholic. This has been the toughest struggle to hit my life, ever. It was the hardest process to understand, the most hurtful experience and the one that has grown me the most of anything else in my life. Different from being born. It has been the sole reason I have realized I needed and started pursuing love for myself, and learning how I must take care of myself before anything else – thanks, therapy! If I can show one person that they are allowed to be wholly grateful for something that completely destroyed them, I have done my work on earth. I have taught myself how to be overwhelmingly grateful to something that sent me on the worst downward spiral of my life. And also learned without loving myself first, I would never dig myself out of that tunnel. I talk about this, because it was the pivotal moment in my life when I started taking full responsibility for my own life, and decided to develop a system for my own life – this was the pivotal moment the twelve steps to self-love was formed, and this book as well, so I feel it is worth at least a mention here. Oh, hey, an accomplishment and acknowledgment, let's have another 30-second dance party.

Why do I think people lack self-love?

Well, because they are not taking responsibility for their own lives. It is a grueling process to acknowledge you are responsible for every single happening in your life. However, if you do not acknowledge and learn to accept this, self-love will be difficult to come by. People are still placing so much responsibility for their happiness, comfort, success, or lack of it, on someone or something else. That moment you start being responsible, you will start to feel the freedom of owning your own life and not taking it for granted. This is where self-love begins. Remember, we are talking about responsibility here – not fault. I'll get into that later.

What are you currently working on; that is bringing you joy?

This book. And my next one floating around in my brain already. This brings me so much joy, because I am able to share what I have learned, developed and applied to my life with others who need it. The words flowed out of me like they had been there all along just waiting for me to recognize my voice.

When you are at peace, what do you do?

I would love to say I am sitting by a quiet lake with a blanket and cup of coffee, taking everything in, just quiet and peaceful. That sounds so dreamy, as it fits to be the correct answer here.

However, much as I would like to make that a reality in the future, it hasn't happened yet. Whenever I am at peace, I am reading a book with a cup of coffee, or sitting in a crowded coffee shop writing, or decorating a Christmas tree with coffee. Basically, if I have a coffee, I am at peace. That is not an attempt at humor; a coffee shop, is apparently my happy place.

What does self-love mean to you, and why is it important?

Self-love to me is being able to take responsibility for yourself. Finding your authentic voice and speaking regardless of who or what may disagree. Being so comfortable with yourself, you no longer seek acceptance or affirmation in others. Knowing who you are at your core and being true to your values. Letting go of toxicity, and breathing intentionally. I could go on, however, there is a whole book here.

Self-love is survival. That is why it is important. It is living. It is everything.

Do you remember the moment you realized how to love yourself?

No! It was a process, it took a lot of time, therapy and yelling. Yes, I am a yeller, I am working on it. The journey to self-love was a steady and regressing process of going back and forth to who I am becoming and who I was. This was never a one moment of experience for me, and it continues to be a journey. And sometimes, I fucked up on something and revert to the old version of who I was, and get to check myself on that.

What does your support system look like?

I have a mentor, a therapist, and incredible group of supportive women, my husband, a spouse addiction support system, a writing partner, a health coach, and a few sprinkles of wonderful friends. I have learned, if someone is not serving and allowing me to be at my greatest good, I get to let go and allow space for someone who does. I have learned when we surround ourselves with people who are out for our greatest good, we will be introduced to more of those people, unless we are holding on to the toxic ones. There will not be space for those who encourage and support us; so, it is time to let go of those we know are not good for us. More of that in the coming chapters.

What is your single most embarrassing moment?

Oh, let's have fun. This is an interesting question, because I feel like there are several. Like the time I was challenged to go live on Facebook and see how many pieces of gum I could fit in my mouth while still talking. Or the time completely ripped my pants at work and had nothing to cover up. Or the time I was doing a Spartan race and couldn't even get over the first wall by myself – the wall that is four feet high and really the challenge to see if you should even be at the start line. Or that time I drunkenly screamed at my best friend at a concert for something that was not even her fault and then tried to apologize later – though that one may be more of shame than embarrassment. I have definitely sent a few texts that were meant for a different recipient, that was always an embarrassment of going too fast, and usually, the person receiving it was the last person you would want to see it. Or the time I busted my ass in front of Target because it was raining, and my flip-flops had no traction. Or the time I passed gas at the airport, loudly. Or all those times I was in a way too much of a hurry and yelled at another driver, or dropped everything, or was sweating like crazy (thanks for those genes grandma). Point made. I have had several embarrassing moments.

How did you embrace your self-perceived flaws?

Again, a process of time. I honestly took one thing at a time, my flaws. My biggest self-perceived flaw is my legs. They are big, and have cellulite, making me uncomfortable. Instead of constantly thinking about what I thought was negative, I simply start to think of all the good shit my legs have done. I have run a half marathon, I have done a few Spartan races, I workout daily, I have walked into some amazing moments and walked away from some awful situations. All with these legs. My legs are a badass when I think of them in those ways, and the more I gave myself this language, the more I started to see them for what they were, instead of what I thought were flaws. I applied this same logic in all areas of my self-perceived flaws. It seems to have worked thus far, so I'll stick with it.

You are going to dinner, where do you go and what do you eat?

Oh, I love talking about food, thinking and devouring it. I would be going to Maggiano's little Italy. I would order their zucchini frittas with their heavenly dipping sauce, I cannot seem to replicate to save my life as an appetizer, their house salad and chicken parmesan with angel hair pasta for dinner. And of course, bread with olive oil for dipping. Pasta is a passion of mine, and I take it seriously.

Do you believe a higher power is at work in your life? If yes; what impact does it have?

Yes! Although, I am not positive what it is. I believe the universe is hard at work in all our lives, and certain things are brought on based on what you put out into the universe, what you give is what you get out of it. I believe some sort of gods are at work in our lives as well – or several of them – though I do not hold the belief of traditional bible teachings. I also feel nature, as it is the most perfect process on Earth, is at work as well and holds a high power in our lives. The main reason I believe connecting with nature is good for our souls.

What is your number one piece of advice for women learning to love themselves?

Take responsibility. That is all! From there, all goods come into your life.That one action will open you up to what you need and are craving in your life. Take responsibility for every single happening, and feeling in your life.

This is me

Amber Haehnel amber@doyouexpedition.com

Chapter 1:

Step1: Acknowledge you have been neglecting and need help accomplishing true love for yourself.

It takes a tribe

The first step to getting anywhere you need to be is acknowledging you need to be there. You get to take that first step, and know you need assistance along the way from other people in the same boat – from other people who have already unpacked those bags you are holding now and have come through on the other side, unpacked and organized, ready to help – or from people who are in the same valley you are currently walking, ready to take your hand and walk through it together up to the mountain top. This is the only way to move forward and become all you were meant to be.

This was particularly difficult for me. Just like the famous line is, "fake it 'til you make it." I thought I was happy, or at the very least I showed other people I was. I put on the fake smile, I did the fake laugh and though sometimes it was real, in rare moments, it made me sad to fake it. I may have been faking it well, but dude, I was so far from making it.

I would continuously body shame myself, and then binge on food, of course, that would make it better. Food was my comfort, my place of solitude, specifically bread. I would have a bad day or see myself in the mirror and realize I had gained some weight, and instead of taking on some personal developments or going to therapy, I would go to bakery therapy and eat until I felt somewhat better mentally and absolutely awful physically. Then, I would look at myself again in the mirror and hate myself more, body shaming myself even more. And the sick carousel continued to spin. But, the pink horse was my favorite and I clung to it for my dear life.

I would put myself down in front of other people, I would make jokes about myself and always thought I was the life of the party. Instead, I was spouting off my insecurities and allowing others to treat me, in the same way, I was treating myself. I had no respect for myself and therefore, even if it was unintentional, others had little respect for me in return. I was opening the door for other people to treat me terribly, exactly the way I had been treating myself. To which, I would go home and grab ahold of that pink horse again.

I would blow up on people. It was awful, I would redirect my self-loathing on to them and assume they either did not like me or just kept me around out of pity. I also projected the expectations of myself on to others, along with my self-doubts, which would make me seem extremely angry most of the time, and believe me, it was not good for my relationships. Being this way left me feeling disappointed in myself, but that was too hard to admit.

I faked it so much, I started to become a chameleon around others. I would adapt to what I thought they wanted me to be. Need someone sophisticated? I got you. Oh, someone who is chill and goes with the flow? No problem, that's totally me. Someone who loves parties and drinking...yep, I've got that down, sister! No matter what the situation, I would adapt myself to what others wanted or needed. And that created some really terrible relationships, cause let's face it, if you are not being true to yourself, you are not happy in the least, and therefore, you are coming off as insincere or fake to others. And the best part? They will begin to treat you this way, so when you finally show your true colors, everything implodes and every type of trust you thought you manifested will have disappeared.

I questioned myself constantly. No matter the situation, I would question my decisions, my thoughts, my actions - all of it. I was never sure of myself, which always came off to other people, never allowing them to get close. If someone did not respond in a matter of minutes, I made up an entire story as to why they hated me, or wracked my brain as to what I did wrong for them to be mad at me. I was constantly wondering if I offended someone, or if I hung out with someone they didn't like and they were mad. And I would lie, if I did not feel like doing something or was too busy, instead of just telling the truth, I would lie and make up plans. This also ended the trust, because the truth will always prevail.

And people pleasing. Oh, friend, that was the absolute worst part of all of this. I was constantly attempting to make someone else happy. Regardless of what I needed or wanted, if someone else needed me; I always said yes to them and no to myself. God forbid, if I

didn't do something, they wouldn't like me or they would be mad at me. Which developed in me coming up with ridiculous excuses, or overbooking myself and therefore overextending myself with no internal benefit in sight. I love making others happy; however, neglecting my own happiness and not setting boundaries was close to literally killing me and my soul. This led to many people knowing they could take advantage of me, and I would go out of my way to do whatever it is they wanted or needed from me, resulting in some terribly toxic relationships with others. And I don't care what else is said on this, when you start to develop only toxic relationships, you really start to develop hateful, negative feelings for people in general. In no time, I started to hate myself and other people, no matter who they were.

All of this obviously took a huge mental toll on me. I was treating myself terribly and developing an awful relationship with the one person I was going to be with forever - myself. I was exhausted, constantly from people pleasing. I was exhausted from being negative constantly – trust me, negativity is extremely exhausting. I was quite possibly addicted to others and depending on them no matter how toxic. I was distraught from never having meaningful conversations and connections with others. I was in a complete freaking mess.

And here goes the crazy talk, I woke up one day and realized I was fucking fed up. This was no way to live, and only I could change that. I started dreaming up ways to remind myself each day that I wanted to be better. That I wanted to get rid of the junk – which may have been the hardest part. I knew a better life was out there, I knew I was meant to be so much more, and I knew something greater was on the horizon. Maybe it was me finally starting to take care of my physical body. Maybe it was the fact that I slowly started to surround myself with more positive people. Maybe it was just in my brain that I could no longer continue the way things were. No one deserves to live an unhappy life.

I did not know it at that time, but I started to develop steps to moving forward. I started researching like a mad woman – and probably applying what I was learning to my life. I took leaps when I didn't think it was possible. I jumped into taking this seriously and knowing my life depended on it. And the Expedition was born. So beautifully and readily.

So, here you are

Acknowledging you need self-love to be the best version of you. Maybe you don't quite know if you deserve it or not (yet), but you know it is essential to growth, and that is the first step in this Expedition of a lifetime.

Look at you; taking that first step is the most important!

Knowing you need help getting there and asking for help from others.

Here are some things you need to know:

We are all in this together. This is a safe place we can share and be vulnerable, and being vulnerable is the key for growth in this process.

There is no judgement. If you find yourself being judgmental, share it, no matter what, because that may be the key to moving forward and owning your own insecurities.

We will work together. Working together, support, bouncing ideas off one another, I strongly encourage you to join up with others, to work through this, or join my group. Again, it takes a tribe.

This is a deep process. It will bring some hard issues to the surface. If it does, we must address these issues/situations in order to grow and move forward. Which brings me to #5.

Trust the process

We get to always choose love first.

This is your expedition – you get to go as fast or as slow as you need to.

Commitment is the key to the door you walk through right this second. You must be willing to commit to yourself and really focus on self-love and growth. This is a marathon, not a sprint. It is going to take time, but if you are committed to self-love, it will happen and be more than worth it. Excuses do not get to live here, and we will push past them together.

At the end of your life, the longest relationship you will have is with yourself. It is the most important.

Without loving yourself first, you cannot and will not be able to fully love others. This is not a selfish practice; it is actually the opposite. By taking care and loving yourself first, you allow yourself to love and give love more freely, and be an all-around better human.

You get to be compassionate with yourself. Treat yourself like you are your own best friend, instead of being your toughest critic. This is easier said than done, and we will work on this. Practice patience with yourself and forgive yourself along the way. This is not a journey of perfection; rather, it is simply linking arms and committing to being a better you today than you were yesterday.

Set healthy boundaries with yourself and others. You get to implement what is healthy for you, and reject what is holding you back. You get to protect your needs and honor your worth. And we go more in depth on how to do this.

Ever heard the old saying, know your value and then add tax? Well, that's what we get to do!

We will be committing to daily acts of self-love – these will be small acts – there is nothing in this expedition too small for you to start doing, in order to be a better you. I will not ask you to spend tons of money, extraordinary amounts of time or sacrifice your life. Cause, let's be real, this is hard; as we already have busy schedules, this gets to be simple and doable. Examples would be waking up and feeling gratitude, or writing in a journal, breathing intentionally for a couple of minutes, moving your phone away from your bed, eliminating the television from the bedroom, etc. One small act to start your day to best benefit your greatest good.

We get to commit to a deep, loving relationship with ourselves and see the positive shift that comes with it.

We get to start from anywhere. There are no limits to who gets to come along with us. I know some of you are sitting back saying, I can never do this, I am not cut out for it, and already thinking up a thousand excuses to get you out of doing this. To be honest with you; this is up to you, whether you listen or move on.

When I started this on my own, I was at the lowest point of my life. I felt worthless from a marriage that was devastating me, and I projected those feelings on to anyone who would sit still with me for more than five minutes. I felt hopeless from so many situations that seemed not to work out. I threw on fake smiles constantly to ward off anyone's questions – which only made me feel worse about myself, that I could pull off fake happy pretty well. I had no clue what my passions were and how to make my dreams come true; so, I tried every single idea I had and ended up looking scattered, rather than put together – and my brain resembled this feeling.

I hated my body. Every inch of it. I had horrible skin, my thighs are huge, my hair just doesn't ever seem to be that perfect mix of shiny and frizz free. My stomach was pudgy and I was out of shape. I tried running and almost threw up.

I projected the lie of hating my body, and only fed myself crap that perpetuated the feelings of hating my body and feeling ashamed.

I once sat and ate an entire pan of brownies because it made me feel better in the moment, only to hate myself more and feel so ashamed I cried myself to sleep – and that wasn't the last time I treated myself that way.

I felt guilty every day, for one thing, or another. I felt like all the deaths that had happened around me was my fault. I constantly felt like someone was mad at me and I needed to fix it immediately, so I tried entirely too hard with people, and I am sure that showed.

Hell, I even felt guilt and shame when I first heard the word cancer. I felt shame that maybe I slept with too many people, or somehow used the wrong product or brought this on myself. I felt guilty for making my family worry about me. I felt awful about the whole thing when in actuality, I should have just been scared and allowed my brain to just be scared. Every single time I heard that word, guilt and shame crept up because I hated myself so much. Which spiraled, because of course my body hated me right back.

I made jokes about myself, so I would feel better, and people wouldn't say them before I could. I made my brain listen to so much nonsense that I finally started believing it. Remember my pink horse. She was always there for me to jump on and allow the carousel to just keep spinning.

My point to all of this, is I am here, right here with you. I know what it feels like to hate yourself, I know what it feels like to be so unhappy but have no idea how to fix it, I know what it feels like to think the entire world has this massive joke and it's about you. I know what this feels like. And that is exactly why I am here.

That is exactly why this book exists, I have been there; hell, I am still there sometimes, and I want to share with you, dear friend, what I did to make it all stop – or at least to make it better. I want to share with you each step I took to get to a better place, to love myself and be a better human, so that maybe you can take some of it and apply to your life, to start living your best life. This is because we all deserved it. More than anything, we deserve to be the best version of us – most of the time anyway – and have a life that is full to the brim and overflowing.

The time is now! We get to take this Expedition and become the person we were meant to be. And they aren't huge, they are small simple steps with slow movement toward that version of us that moves mountains, and show others how it's done.

And it all starts here, acknowledging you need to be a better version of you, move past the terrible, and on to the future. Admitting you need to better handle the current situations, and say no to what doesn't matter, let go of the shit storm of the past and come into the light. Acknowledging you get to take the steps forward and having a tribe of people with your greatest good at their forefronts, because you have theirs in yours. Admitting you need to link arms with others and have a massive impact on this earth, just by being your true self.

Acknowledging you deserve self-love, because it is the ultimate love, and my friend, you deserve all of it.

I am thrilled you are here.

Reflection:

- What do I get to change?
- What will the repercussions be if I do not change?
- What pain or fear do I associate with self-love?
- What are the benefits I will get from this change?
- How have I made myself unhappy?
- How have I tried to change in the past? What has worked/not worked?
- Am I willing to do whatever it takes to change my mindset and how I treat myself?

Featured Female – Stephanie Hallman

This is ME

Stephanie and I met because I had previously worked with her partner, James. We developed a working relationship with her, creating gorgeous vinyl pieces for my woodworking, and even further blossomed into a wonderful friendship. She is a mom, a dog mom, a fearless advocate for Pregnancy and Infant Loss Awareness – having suffered that loss herself, a partner, a loyal friend and the owner/operator of an amazing company, Vinylerapy – where her art is her therapy. Her life story and the story of her work are incredible, and I am so grateful to share her with you here.

Who are you as a human?

Perfectly imperfect. I am full of all kinds of flaws and even go to therapy sessions. Yep, it's all part of my self-love regimen. If I am not healthy on all levels, I cannot care for my family properly. You can't pour from an empty cup! Self-care is an act of self-love. I am usually a hot mess juggling lots of different hats. I live by a daily checklist and calendar; learning to take charge of my day by slowing down its speed. Life is hectic, and can zoom right by you if not harnessed. I am a student learning to stop and smell the roses! And yes, I place my self- love acts on my daily checklists.

What do you do for a living? Why do you choose it?

I run a small T-shirt and vinyl decal business called Vinylerapy – a little play on words there – vinyl is my therapy. I couldn't imagine myself doing anything else. It all started with a safari will design for my teenage son's bedroom. My fiancés' amazing mom mentioned I should start a business using my creative talents. After networking a bit, I began creating decals for various non-profit foundations supporting Pregnancy and Infant Loss Awareness (PAILA) – A topic that has touched my heart deeply. From there, my business flourished and blossomed into what it is today. I still work off my family's dining room table, but it is perfect for me! Art is life!

Why do you think people lack self-love?

Society. I think our society is cruel. I had to disconnect from the outside world for a little while – dial it back to just me for a bit. I spent a lot of time soul searching until I discovered who I really am, and slowly brought people back into my life that serve me and my life intentions – and not serve like cater to me, but serve like on my path of a healthy me. I was able to leave the poisonous people in the dark – YOU KNOW WHO I MEAN! I only let in love and light – those who carry the same vibe as me. Anyhow, a one-word answer – Society.

When you are at peace what are you doing? What does that look like?

Meditating. For those of you who do it – YOU KNOW WHAT I MEAN! And for those of you who don't, give it a shot!

Learning to breathe – like really focusing on my breathing – has quieted my mind so very much. A 30-minute meditation session to me is better than a night of sleep. It frees my mind from clutter. It is like a power-nap! I'm refreshed and completely rejuvenated. Seriously – TRY IT!

What does self-love mean to you?

To me, self-love is a series of acts that cleanse the mind, body and soul, to ensure you are running like a well-oiled machine! Also, let me refer to my answer on the importance of self-love.

Why do you think self-love is important?

To me, self-love is important because it is the foundation of who you really are – like the REAL you! Seriously, you may THINK you know yourself, but after a solid regimen of self-love, you will see that you blossomed into this RAY OF SUNSHINE – ok, so it's a little dramatic, but seriously, it will feel good to truly feel good; as you will wonder why you waited so long to practice self-care.

Do you remember the moment you realized how to love yourself? Will you share that experience?

Nope, it was a process. I am not sure there was a true 'moment,' but a series of moments that helped me realize I was on the right path.

What does your support system look like?

Two friends. I sometimes veer off course and it takes me a bit to recover – I'm only human and full of flaws. When this occurs, I have two very special friends I turn towards to assist in my recovery. These two friends, Julie and Jennifer, don't just tell me what I want to hear; instead, they explain things from a clear unboggled mind. Both are true friends that know where my mind goes, and they know how to reel me back in with their point of views. They ALWAYS get me back on track and gets my head back in the game!

How did you embrace your self-perceived flaws?

For starters, no one is perfect. Furthermore, define perfect. Your idea of perfection is going to be completely different from mine, I assure you. And with that being said, just stop trying to be something else and just learn to love you for the wonderful human you are! I think it's important to understand your self-perceived flaws, so you know how to tackle them when they come rearing their ugly heads! Write a letter to yourself – sounds silly, I know. But seriously, write a note to yourself listing several things you beat yourself up about and then follow each excerpt with encouraging words. Don't let crazy talk keep you from getting back up when you fall. And keep that letter handy. I think it's important to remember I reach out to my support system – Julie and Jennifer. Those ladies keep my head on straight and help me get back up!

You are going to dinner...where do you go and what do you eat?

I love Sharkey's! It's a wonderful little organic Mexican grill here in Las Vegas. Fresh, nutrient-packed, locally grown food! Yum! I ordered a Baja Shrimp Taco (sometimes two) with rice and black beans (vegan so no yucky lard added).

Do you believe a higher power is at work in your life? What impact does that have?

I am spiritual, but not religious. I do believe in a higher power and strive to elevate myself. I am becoming more spiritual as I become older, realizing that my thoughts and state of mind greatly affect my position in life. I believe in myself. When I pray, I am really reaching deep within to find the resolution. I have the power within to solve any dilemma and by doing so with such confidence means I will not limit myself. I believe in me.

What is your number one piece of advice for women learning to love themselves?

Make a daily checklist – start with one daily task, and do it for a week. Try something simple like "smiling more." It may seem silly to place this on your

Checklist, but do it anyway. Throughout the day, ask yourself if you could smile more. It's a joyous feeling that makes you warm and fuzzy on the inside and it's contagious. Week Two – add another item to your checklist – 1) smile more 2) compliment yourself. Take a moment after washing your hands in the restroom and look into your beautiful eyes and smile; then, tell yourself

something nice. "great makeup application" – "snazzy accessorizing" – "damn, that's a good hair day!" – "nice job not throat punching Susie earlier!" LOVE YOURSELF! Be kind to yourself! Learn to say NO! Your body is your temple – Feed it like a queen (eat healthy!) Remove poisonous people! Smile – a lot! This list goes on…

How can women connect with you?

Email: sbhallman@hotmail.com

Facebook: Stephanie Hallman &/or Vinylerapy

Chapter 2:

Step 2: Be willing to make a change in yourself.

You get to be the change you wish to see.

If it is to be, it is up to you. No one else wants or cares about your dreams, hopes, fears, love, and attitude more than you. No one! It's a hard truth, but that's the reality. You are the only person who is going to care about everything in your life, and no one else can make you change, it is all up to you. There is no other person who can make you happy, give your dreams life, or step up to the plate.

It's a go time, darling. If you wish to change your life, it is all on you. No matter what you want life to look like or how you want to manage it, it is solely your responsibility to get there.

It took me quite a long time to become willing enough to actually make a change. After all of my research, I knew I needed to, but doing it was another story. I acted like I knew what was up, I was a genius in this realm and had it all figured out. I quickly realized I was so good at faking it to make it, I was faking this as well. I would read the books, post it on social media and absorb the information like a sponge, but never actually apply any of it. But hey, everyone on social media saw me reading the book, so I must be making changes, right?! Of course, social media is life; so, that is what mattered, my highlight reel.

I had to have long conversations with myself, I had to get angry and curse at myself, I had to have other people point it out to me, I had to get frustrated all before I would be willing to actually make it happen and apply all I was learning. It takes a tribe, and at that time, my tribe were books and research, neither of which will make you get off your ass and get it done – more on that in step 3.

I am explaining my experience, because I want to acknowledge that not one bit of this process is easy, and you may think you have it all under control, hell, you may even look like you have it all under control. It takes energy, effort and grit to make this happen, and to start. I acknowledge and appreciate all of that on this Expedition. You are not unnoticed, and you have to be fully willing, all the way to be here. Take your time, we will be here when you are ready.

Ready? Set. Go!

Letting go

The first action we get to take is that of letting go. In order to fully practice self-love and be present in this expedition, you get to let go of anything and everything holding you back.

You get to eliminate the who's, the what's, the when's and the how's that are keeping you from being your true identity. - paraphrasing from the perfection, that is Mr. Mathew McConaughey.

This means those friends and family who doubt you or question the decisions you are making. The people who don't truly believe you have what it takes, the ones that call you crazy for chasing after something. The ones who are worried about you and the decisions you are making. The ones who will never take the leap themselves and therefore do not want you to take that leap. At the end of this, they are not seeing how capable they are. They don't want to lose you, and they are scared; which is alright and honestly natural. However, you are no longer going to allow their fear to become yours. Let's read that all over again – you are not going to allow their fear to become yours. This does not mean you write them off completely, but you get to make decisions on who you spend the most of your time with, in order to become your best self, and I'll tell you, it is not these people. Don't worry, in my experience, these types of relationships tend to organically drift as you move forward. It may be painful and stressful, but not as much as you are thinking, this I promise.

This also means anything in your home that you do not believe to be beautiful or helpful. Anything in your home that is not serving your greatest good. That crock pot of your grandmothers you haven't used in 5 years...out it goes. The fake plant collecting dust on the shelf, no longer! The dress you bought 3 years ago with the tag "might fit into one day," donate that to someone who will actually rock it! The dress deserves it. Better yet, sell it! That box of old shit from past lovers?! Gone! *This shouldn't even be a thought, get rid of it. It is not serving you to have sentimental items of the past, especially when they usually are worse for your heart than they are good for it.

Truly go through your home with that intention and say goodbye to those things. You will feel lighter as you go. You will have an uplifting feeling as you are able to let things go. At the end of the day, we are not defined by our things, have the courage to toss or donate what you do not need around you.

Stop buying things you don't need, with money you don't have to impress people you don't like – the wonder that Mr. Dave Ramsey said and it has clung to me since I read it.

We will dig into this much more in a later step, for now, take the basics and start.

Warning: Do not put this off. This is an easy task to push off to another day, or push off to when you have time to host a garage sale. You can have a virtual garage sale these days, take advantage. If it doesn't sell in 3 days, donate it. You need these things gone to truly start out an expedition of love.

June Carter used to give away books after she read them to lighten her load – or at least that was her action in the movie – either way, a great lesson, take a hint from her and lighten that load. You may even be able to help someone else in the process. You know the saying; your junk is more than likely someone else's treasure.

The Big Moment

Are you truly ready to change? Do you really believe you are deserving of self-love? This is because you also get to let go of the judgement.

Once upon a time, I was heavily judged for even practicing self-love, I was called selfish, a time waster, weird, you get the idea. You may also be called selfish or judged wrongly, and if you are not truly ready to stand in the purpose and intention of self-love, you may let this sway you from continuing.

Stand in purpose and intention, knowing you deserve this and will be a better human once you make the commitment. This will help you to do away with those who are not ready for the expedition and judging you for it.

Lose all doubts about the process. You get to stand in an entirely new perspective of life, if there are any doubts, this can be accomplished as we get to return to step 1. And this is your journey, you are allowed to return to any step at any time if it is what you need.

This process will be difficult; it may be the most challenging time you will ever have. I return to the statement that your relationship with yourself will be the longest and most important in your life.

It will also take time and investment, and the more time and energy you invest into yourself, the more you will see in return.

That is how energy works, the more you give, the more you get. How much are you willing to give, if your life depends on it?

How do you rid yourself of judgement? Well, you practice a shit ton of patience. You start telling yourself truths about what you are judging. That lady at the grocery store with loud kids? Maybe she just lost her mom and is losing her patience. The friend that keeps cancelling? Maybe they are going through a difficult time and do not want to talk about it. The guy at the stop light with a "need food" sign? Maybe he has lost all of his family and just lost his job, when he was already two paychecks behind. Start practicing gratitude, for example, I am so grateful, so I have someone to watch the kids, so I can run to the store, I am grateful for friends that I enjoy spending time with when we are available, I am so grateful to have the money in my account and a roof over my head. Practice gratitude each time you feel judgmental and you will notice it becoming a habit and dropping the judgement. And you will notice this for the judgements you make about yourself as well.

Excuses

How many times have you broken a promise to yourself, or given up on yourself to watch television? I heard this statement and it stopped me dead in my tracks. This is because I cannot count how many times I have allowed this to happen.

I will repeat, excuses just don't live here. I want you to take a moment and think about all the excuses you have given, just over the past week. How could you have eliminated the excuse?

I don't have time, is one of my favorites and most loathed excuses. And I am calling bullshit on anyone who uses this excuse. So, this is the practice you get to begin. Instead of saying I don't have time, replace those words with it's not a priority, and see how actions change. This was a powerful statement for myself. Think about it, I don't have time to have sex with my partner – swap that for it's not a priority to have sex with my husband. Excuse me, what? I don't have time to prepare healthy meals for my family – it is not a priority to create healthy meals for my family. Damn, sister. Really not cool when you begin to word it that way, and you may be able to flip the script and see what you really do have time for, if you eliminate time-wasting activities. You really don't have time to complain about the phone with a girlfriend for an hour, that is what you don't have time for. Except, you have made that a priority, and the other two examples should be much more of a priority for you than complaining about anything – regardless of the content or who you are complaining to. Think about making a television show a priority over doing a workout. You are feeding your brain junk – please, don't get me wrong, I actually love – instead of fueling your body to make it perform at its best. Priorities, people! Get them in check, and use this to not only do that, but also to eliminate that annoying time excuse.

Excuses come up when we are not passionate about what we are doing with our lives, when it is not a priority in our lives, or is not something we WANT to be doing. An excuse is your brain being frightened. Your brain is a tricky organ, it enjoys the regular and mundane, because that is what it is used to. When you throw in something new, exciting or not, your brain reacts in a way as if to say, hold up! I don't like new, what are we going to do with that, I don't know how to manage that. This is why we get nervous, scared, excited, shake like crazy, fearful, you know the feeling. Just before you are about to talk in front of someone, or on a first date. You get to push past these feelings.

Mel Robbins wrote about the 5 seconds rule – which I highly recommend – and the prefrontal cortex, the part of your brain that reacts in the description above, to trick your brain into moving in a different direction when something new is brought into the mix. Taking five seconds to decide on something really works, and allows you to jump without the fear in your brain taking over. But, I digress, grab the book and read it for yourself.

I hear it all the time – when I lose weight, when I have the time, when I find a job I love, when I get rid of this acne (guilty), when I fall in love, etc., then I will work on myself and try to love myself. Here's a newsflash: You will not accomplish any of this and be happy, if you don't love yourself now, for exactly who you are. Without true love for yourself, none of these things will matter, and you will not give them all you have unless you love yourself first. You cannot wish your damn self into self-love – you have to work to get there, and there is no outside influence that will help – it comes from within you and only you. There is no source outside of yourself who will change the way you currently feel about you. No job, weight, status, friends, or mate will make you feel love for yourself. It might trick you for a brief period of time, but it will not be lasting love unless you do it for yourself.

You no longer get to give yourself excuses. Excuses will not get results, believe me, I have tried on several occasions, I have tried every single way to make excuses. In short, I've been there, I've made that excuse, so don't even try it with me, my love, I will knock it down so fast you will be stumbling with your words trying to think of another before I knock that one away with the wind as well. Take this seriously, excuses cannot live here anymore.

My advice to giving up excuses would be to flip it. Whenever you have a thought of not doing something you know needs to happen to get you to where you need to be, flip it. I don't have time/it's not a priority, I am tired/I have all the energy I need, I had a long day/I still have several hours to accomplish one thing, I am so busy/I always have time for what matters, I don't want to/I want to live my dream life and nothing will stop me, I'm not good enough/I excel in my life, I don't have the money/I have an amazing relationship with money and it flows to and from me freely; you get the point, flip that script on your excuses and you begin forming a brand new mindset.

Create a routine, and stick to it for at least one week. Whether it is getting up early or staying up a little later, or maybe not watching so much television to ensure you get at least one hour to work on yourself per day. I am certain if you search hard enough, you will find an hour, even if that hour is in fifteen-minute increments. My friend, if you do not have an hour a day for yourself, you are certainly not living much of a life, and we get to start over. It is there, seek it out and use it to your advantage.

You will make time for what is important, you will say no to what does not serve you, and you will push forward with what you truly want. You get to do all of this for yourself.

How beautiful is that?! And how freeing it will be to let go of excuses and start living.

Reflections:

- Do I accept that I get to think/feel/act differently?
- Am I willing to let go of what does not serve me and do it quickly? What am I letting go?
- How will I give up the comfort of my excuses?
- What are my doubts about this expedition? How do I get to address these?
- Am I having trouble in exterior relationships in my life?
- Am I lacking purpose and drive? How?
- What fear am I experiencing with this expedition?

Featured Female – Jenna Curnutte

This is ME

Jenna and I met online, the joys of social media connection. We were a part of a larger fitness group and finally met at a retreat a year after our online meeting. I was drawn to Jenna immediately, her sunny disposition and how she has the ability to tell it like it is. I was so envious of that quality, and knew I could count on her to give me sound, tough but loving advice when necessary.

She is a mom, a wife, a Coach and helps women navigate through the uncertainties of new motherhood like a boss. Her passion is felt hard in everything she does.

Who are you as a human?

I am a wife, mother, daughter and sister. I am a teacher, a creator, a Christian, and an entrepreneur. I am loving, caring and confident. I am scared, fearful and ever changing.

What do you do for a living? Why do you choose it?

I chose to be a mother for a living and while that is my dream job, we needed extra income. I chose not to leave my son, and instead create a business I can run from home. I sell teething items for babies and coach moms to be their most confident selves in all areas of their lives.

Why do you think people lack self-love?

Society has put so many expectations and restrictions on people, especially women. We are filled with self-doubt, in constant fear of what others think or say about us. We worry more how we look on the outside to others rather than how we look on the inside to ourselves. It is easier to live in fear than live in power.

What are you currently working on that is bringing you joy?

I am currently creating my line of teething toys and necklaces to sustain our stay at home life. Being home with my son brings me joy and being able to do something I truly love makes my dream that much sweeter. Supporting moms and babies continue to fill my life with joy.

When you are at peace what are you doing? What does that look like?

Sleeping! Haha. No for real, moms are tired AF. And naps are our happy place!

Truly, what brings me peace right is my son playing, Hallmark Christmas movies in the background, and building my legacy, one bead, one word, one connection at a time. Being home is my peaceful place. My other favorite place, when I'm at peace is singing in the church. Worshipping and being with my family.

What does self-love mean to you?

Self-love means being selfish. Putting me first. Putting my needs first.

Whether it is cleaning the fridge, soaking in a bath, getting my nails done, or hitting snooze for the eight times. Self-love can be anything that I need at that moment. And it's crucial for sanity.

Why do you think self-love is important?

Self-love is important to create a balance in your life, in your mind, and in your soul. It sounds cheesy, but without self-love, you don't have the clarity to give the areas of your life the attention they needed. Putting on your oxygen mask first is important, so that you are able to help everyone else around you.

Do you remember the moment you realized how to love yourself? Will you share that experience?

Unfortunately, I do not. I am not sure if it's because I don't remember my childhood or because I am still learning how to love myself. It's a forever journey. And it's like a muscle you get to exercise daily, so it doesn't get weak.

What does your support system look like?

I'm growing my support system to be an inner circle I truly trust. In the past, I had kept friends because I was scared of losing them and being alone. I was the friend everyone wanted. Loyal, and kind, but I never had friends who would do that for me. But now, I am surrounded by amazing women who lift me up and support me. Who truly cares about me. Although, I am still learning to lean on them, but am blessed and grateful for who I call a friend.

Outside of my amazing Mentorship group, I have my husband as a great support system and his so encouraging. My mom and brothers are awesome too. I truly have an incredible family who loves and supports my dreams.

Tell me about your journey to love

I am sorry, but if I must be honest with you; I am a perfectionist. I used to starve myself to lose weight, I used to drown in diet pills and cigarettes. I took everything personally and felt like I was never good enough. I used sex to keep guys around and drank so much the bartenders knew me by name. I wasn't terrible. But I had no respect or love for myself.

My confidence is something I am forever in the process of developing and I'm learning to love who I am, the better version of me, every single day. I believe loving yourself is a journey with no final destination.

What is your single most embarrassing moment?

I don't believe I have one. Nothing that comes to mind as incredibly embarrassing. Not outwardly at least.

How did you embrace your self-perceived flaws?

I'm uniquely myself. I truly don't think I could have embraced who I am without the support and love of women who do not compare but instead empower.

You are at dinner…. where do you go and what do you eat?

I hate making decisions!!!! I'd have to say, Wine Guy. Sip some Ras di Roas and enjoy appetizers.

Do you believe a higher power is at work in your life? What impact does that have?

Yes. I believe God has a plan for my life and everything that happens to me is for a reason. I know he created me in his perfect image, loves my flaws and all. It brings peace to my life to know a love that grand.

What is your number one piece of advice for women learning to love themselves?

Planning your day and being intentional is the most important. Make your schedule dictates your life and mind. Begin your day with gratitude. Find positivity in every situation. Do something that is for YOU. Organize your mind and life so that you get the most out of each day.

How can women connect with you?

Email: confidentmamacoaching@gmail.com
Website: www.confidentmamacoaching.com
Facebook: Jenna Curnutte

Chapter 3:

Step 3 – Are you willing to accept help along this expedition, and honestly tell someone you trust that you are starting this expedition?

Well, you are here. You made it this far.

Maybe you didn't think this is what it would be about, maybe you did and know you need a tribe to help you along, maybe you just wanted to jump in and see what would happen, but here you are.

That's a start, you are starting. Give yourself a small pat. In this expedition, we get to celebrate all the wins!

A Trusted Confidant.

The time we get to brainstorm, and really dig deep to find someone you trust completely. You get to tell them about the expedition you have decided to jump into, and ask them to hold you accountable. This gets to be someone who will not judge, who will accept this expedition and be supportive – also, someone who will allow you to check in and keep you on track. If we keep this a secret, there will be no accountability, and therefore not a lot of progress. As humans, we need accountability to succeed.

Dig deep on your feelings. Are you feeling depressed, emotionally drained, stressed, or fatigued?

You get to tell your person all of this. The perfect person may be someone on this expedition as well, or it may be someone far from it, find someone who works you, there is no right or wrong answer, so long as you decided based on your needs. This person may change several times over the course of your expedition, which is totally ok, as well. And this gets to be reciprocal, if they are not on this expedition, find a way to be of service to them as they are of service to you.

Acknowledge, if what you have done in the past has not worked, and commit to trusting this process. Had your previous attempts worked, there would be no need to start an expedition, and you wouldn't be here.

My person came to me right away, and I immediately let her know what the deal was. She was supportive and tough; although, she did not understand, she vowed to support me through this. She was instrumental in getting me where I needed to be. I was honest with her, allowing her to be honest with me, while I understood her responses were not judgmental but instead challenging, which allowed me to reflect and apply ideas to my life, instead of just listening and moving on. I will be forever grateful for her involvement in my expedition.

However, this is not to say that different seasons in your life won't require different types of people. After a while, I realized I was changing seasons in my life and she was no longer able to be my person. This may or may not happen to you, but it is ok regardless. If you feel the person you originally chose can no longer serve you in the way you need, chose another. It is about your expedition and what is going to work best for you, do not…I repeat, do not feel guilty about that. Some people serve you amazingly in one season and tend to drift off in the next. That is life, and it is perfectly fine. Be gentle with letting your person go and remain to be there for them. Your season changing does not need to be negative in their life.

My next choice did not come easily. I learned some lessons and looked for different qualities. I analyzed everything because I wanted my next person to be there for life – which may or may not be the case with yours. I was overdoing it. I was not going to find my person this way. So, I let go of my expectations, and approached a friend I was unsure about. She gave a resounding yes and decided to go along with me on the ride. Sometimes, it just works that way. I recommend you let go and let your heart take you where it needs to be, it may take some time, but you will find the correct person, and that person is more likely to be there for life.

And since it is my book, I get to insert my own opinion when I feel necessary – that would be now. For me, my spouse was not going to be this person for me. At first, he was not comprehending what the hell I was doing, nor was he interested. He just figured, be happy if you want to be happy, he didn't understand. And honestly, sometimes the frustration and hurt I was attempting to move past were about him, so I could not choose him to discuss this with and connect with on the expedition, he was simply too close to the situation. It just did not make sense to me to have him as my person here. He is my person pretty much everywhere else, so this one was on me. I also knew if I allowed him into this expedition, it would become more of him or us, and I needed this to be about me and mine alone. To do this on my own, for myself and no one else. In this case, it was just not going to be him. I recommend you take stock of asking a spouse, partner, close family member, as you may not be as honest as you need to be, and you may start doing things for the wrong reasons. Allow this to be yours. If these people are able to do that for you, fantastic! If not, seek out someone else.

When you do find your person, I suggest telling him/her you are on an expedition of self-love and doing a twelve-step based program, and you would like to inform him/her of the work you are doing and check in with him/her weekly to update on progress. You get to give them permission to hold you accountable, call you out and give you tough love. You get to take it when they give you these things – do not, I repeat, do not take this personal, as it is detrimental to this process.

And if you need access to a larger community, join mine!!!

Choose wisely sister, and update! Here are the reasons we need a partner or a community in this process...

Pride

We get to talk about pride here, in other words, how do you think others think about you? Tongue twister, eh? I want you to learn this mantra and say it to yourself over and over, until it sticks like pasta to the wall:

What others think of me is none of my business.

We get to find out our true selves, and that means letting go of what others think of how you live your life, how you look and what you do. You are no longer living for anyone else. How freaking freeing and empowering is that?! Please, let it be. You get to live solely on purpose for yourself.

I appreciate that this is not an easy task, it takes time to restructure the way your brain works. Most of us have spent years thinking and acting a certain way – it takes time and a whole lot of effort to change that. In order to live fully for yourself, it is a must. After all, when people are judgmental, they are not protecting you, they are protecting themselves. Humans have an innate fear of what they do not understand, and what they do not want to change. They don't want you to change, or they are scared to change themselves; therefore, they try to keep you the same. In the same boring, non-loving place where you have been unhappy. No more! You get to take hold of the reins.

And it is none of your business what other people think of you, that is up to them....and try as you might, there will be no changing on that. Just as this expedition is all about you, their judgements and fear are theirs – not yours. Just let them go!

I appreciate this is not an easy task, you get to practice one day at a time, focusing on you and moving past the opinions of others. How? Embarrass yourself. Go out and embarrass yourself, right now. The more you do it, the more you realize how little you care about other people's thoughts and how good it feels to simply be you.

Self esteem

Yep, we get to talk about the old self esteem. What you think of yourself. This is detrimental to the outcome of your self-love, they go hand in hand. What you think of yourself, even if you do not speak it out loud, is what you are. If you think you are fat, lazy, unattractive, unqualified, then you are. Get it? If you recalculate your thoughts around how awesome you are, the fact that you have special gifts the world needs, that you are beautiful, then that is how you will start to think of yourself.

This one takes some time also. Work with it.

Self-love and self-esteem are partners in crime, they get each other and they work together. You get to have both on this journey! Take some time to review your thoughts of yourself – whether you voice them or not. How are they serving you, and how can they better serve you? How do you get to rework your self-esteem to be your right hand man on this expedition?

Relationships

This is where trusting friends come in. They get to be your person, the person you go to when you need a kick in the ass, so they also get to be tough, and you get to take it when they are.

See how important picking out a good one is for this exercise?

You get to tell them the script you have been telling others, no matter what it is. And you also get to rewrite that script.

For years, I struggled with being a pushed over, and allowing other people to know that and take advantage of me. These are not friends; this is not someone I want in my life (refer to dropping what doesn't serve you). I struggled with how to change that script, how do I start telling people no? How I do all of a sudden change how I respond to people? Well, you just have to do it. It's that simple! You just change and allow those who support that change – see above, what was written on Pride. Again, this is not an easy task and I appreciate that. However, it is a necessary task to becoming who you truly are.

You and you alone are in control of your script, write it well, tell it well and tell it honestly. The more vulnerable and honest you are, the more you will attract honesty in your life, and the more dishonesty will fall away naturally.

Ambitions

Oh, the old ambition. It's there; sometimes, it just needs to be brought back to the surface. Think of what you wanted to do as a child, what your plans were for the future. As children, we do not think about failure, we simply get to dream for ourselves, and that is where ambition derives from. From the roots of our visions as children. We could dream, and imagine infinite possibilities of where our lives would go, and no one person could tell us otherwise. Let's bring this back to the surface of our being. Screw what anyone else says, what do you truly want to do? Who do you truly want to be? Take it back old school, bust out the jams and get to thinking, without anyone telling you otherwise.

Think about it, no decent human tells a child they cannot live out their dreams, that would just be awful. I mean, I am sure it happens, but for the most part, children get to just live and dream and imagine the world as this infinite place of possibilities. Get back to that. Who gives a shit if someone else thinks you can't, or thinks you are crazy – it is not their life, it is yours. Are you really going to let someone else's opinion stops you from being true to yourself? I certainly hope not.

Dream it up, take some time and think of what you truly want out of life, regardless of what anyone would think of you.

Reflections:

- What does your ideal person look like?
- What values does your person hold?
- What is your overall vision for your life?
- How does the perfect version of you look?
- What did you want to be when you grow up?

This part does not come easy or quickly; so, take time to really dig deep on these questions and design a life you get to be proud of.

Questions to determine the right person for this job:

- How did we meet?
- Do I completely trust this person?
- Do I feel comfortable speaking openly and honestly with this person?
- What qualities do they possess that I find will be helpful?
- Have I ever found myself feeling judged by them?
- Have they been working on themselves as well?
- What is our connection?

Some tips on this:

I found that this person may be someone who is close to you, but not too close, I would highly suggest not having a parent or spouse be this person for you. They love you and want to support you; however, trust you are starting this expedition

they also have their agenda and thoughts about how you should be living your life, therefore, they will be a bit biased, even unintentionally.

Build trust with this person, by first explaining what this is about and what you will be needing from them during this time, and ask if they are comfortable with that?

Featured Female – Britt Fields

This is ME

I first met Britt at work, which seems like about a million lifetimes ago. First things I noticed? Her incredible hair, smile and positive attitude. At the same

time, I knew she would tell it like it is, she was not a delicate human and she could take it just as easy as she could dish it out. I was envious of the person she was, so sure of herself. Over the years, we stayed connected – thanks to social media – and I have watched her discipline for fitness into something awesome. The thing I remembered most about our conversations, she once told me, anything she tries, she turns it into an experiment with herself to stick to it (i.e, diet). I took that to heart. She is an incredible human. I knew I had to have her voice represented here.

Who are you as a human?

I am confident, strong and independent. I am blunt and outspoken with an inappropriate sense of humor. I tend to set goals and go after them with everything I have. I am always striving to improve in every aspect of my life.

What do you do for a living and why did you choose it?

I am a Medical Laboratory Scientist. I chose this career because I have a natural talent for science and math; I love being in the laboratory. I am a person who likes details and needs evidence with lots of information before I come to a conclusion. I have always been fascinated by science at the microscopic level and also pathology.

Why do you think people lack self-love?

Comparison. There is too much comparing of oneself to others. Not only as individuals, but as a society at large. Women are constantly being compared to each other and portrayed a certain way. People are expected to behave a certain way and live a certain way, etc. It's as if we can't be ourselves or be confident in ourselves. How can you have self-love if you can't even be yourself?

What are you currently working on that is bringing you joy?

Bodybuilding. I just obtained my IFBB Pro Card in Figure, and now, I am currently sculpting my physique, so that I can one day make it to the Arnold and Olympia.

When you are at peace; what are you doing? What does that look like?

I am most at peace when I am at the gym. I can let go of all my frustrations and obligations, and focus only on the task at hand.

It's a stress reliever and also my happy place. And a nice little bonus to that is increased athleticism, strength and better health.

What does self-love mean to you?

Self-love is loving yourself unconditionally. You can love yourself while improving yourself. You can love yourself at every moment, even if you are in the middle of whatever goal. It is loving yourself through every stage of your journey.

Why do you think self-love is important?

Self-love is probably the most important thing a person can have. If you have self-love, you have confidence. You have the confidence to go after your goals, you take care of yourself, body and mind. If you have self-love, you have the ability to love others and care for others the way you would for yourself.

Do you remember the moment you realized how to love yourself? Will you share that experience?

It isn't one moment. I gained most of confidence and self-love through bodybuilding for sure. Going against social norms made me a target for criticism. I knew what I wanted to do, despite getting pushback from others.

The more confident I became, not only in myself but also in what I wanted to achieve, the more I learned to care less about what others think. I learned their

opinions don't matter. My opinion about myself is what matters. I learned that I am capable of so much, despite being different, and looking different. I can't be compared because I am unique. I learned to love myself and it transferred to every other area of my life: my job, my friendships, my happiness, and my relationships.

What does your support system look like?

My support system is small. I have my sister and my father. My father is my world and had a huge influence on me and the person I am today. My father is my everything. My gym and the members there is also a support system. They are there to cheer for me when I compete, they help me get going on days when I felt down.

What is your single most embarrassing moment?

I don't think I have a single most embarrassing moment. I've embarrassed myself numerous times, but looking back, they were learning experiences. E.g. I lost horribly at a bodybuilding competition and I started to pout and act like a brat. Luckily my coach was there and pointed out my behavior, and told me I needed to have better sportsmanship. He did this (respectfully) in front of a few others, but it made me realize I needed to handle losses better and focus on improving instead of pouting.

How did you embrace your self-perceived flaws?

I made my flaws my strengths. Physically, I have always had big legs and I always hated them. I didn't want them any bigger. I started bodybuilding and had to make them bigger, and stronger. Now, my legs are a huge strength in competitions. My sarcasm, sense of humor and bluntness were also what I thought of as flaws. But now, I see them as strengths. I'm hyper and bubbly, and can make light a lot of things. But I am also very real and open with my feelings, I'm honest. I may lack tact at times, but no one has to wonder what I'm feeling or if I'm telling the truth or not.

You are going to dinner…where do you go and what do you eat?

Umami Sushi! Sushi is my all-time favorite.

Do you believe a higher power is at work in your life? What impact does that have?

I am an atheist. My accomplishments are my own. I worked hard to achieve my goals, with the support of friend and family, of course. I sacrificed, dedicated the time, had the discipline even when I lacked motivation.

What is your number one piece of advice for women learning to love themselves?

Hype yourself up! Stop talking negatively about yourself. When you have a negative thought about yourself, think "would I say this to a friend?" probably not. You should treat yourself the way you would treat any person you love. I talk to myself all the time! When I'm nervous or think I'm not good enough

or when I compare, I stop myself and turn it around. I tell myself "I deserve to be here, I worked hard for this, I am capable, I am worthy."

How can women connect with you?

Instgram: @brittfitscientist

Email: brittfitscientist@gmail.com

Chapter 4:

Step 4 – Write down all of your limiting beliefs, insecurities and self-doubts – do not leave anything out.

Are you ready for the fun?

This is my favorite step, most likely because it was the hardest for me to accomplish. It wasn't easy, friends. But I love the challenge, and you may not; however, the future is now. This was the turning point in my expedition, and I jumped head first in on this step. I hadn't realized at the time I dove head first into a wading pool and damn near broke my face, but it turned out fine, and it was worth it. Again, this one is hard. We can do hard things (keep that on repeat for a while until it's burned in your mind).

Limiting beliefs are a series of false beliefs you think about yourself - a.k.a horse shit, and quite difficult to change. We have most likely been telling ourselves these stories for a long time, years even; so, it will not be easy to transition into changing them; however, it is not impossible. Some of my favorites – and most frustrating - limiting belief examples:

- I don't have enough money.
- I can't do that.
- I am not qualified enough.
- I am not nearly as happy as that.

All false...all crap our brains tell us to keep us from doing something different and strange. Keeping us from doing something that could dramatically impact our lives. Brains are funny that way, they like the mundane, they really do not like change; hence, the reason it is easier to just continue to believe these things about ourselves instead of changing them. It is easier to stay the same, however, it is not worth it. I repeat, you can do hard things.

Limiting beliefs sometimes show up as excuses: back to the classic, I don't have time. When limiting beliefs show up as excuses, it is much easier to just allow them to take over your whole life. Excuses are easy to come by, mostly because the action causing the excuse is something we do not particularly find exciting or fun. Until now.

Think about your last workout, did you want to do it? Did you try like hell to find a way out of it? I am going to go ahead and guess the answer is yes. Now, think about the last time you went to a theme park, or planned an exciting night out or went to your favorite restaurant…were you making excuses then? I would assume the answer is no here, because it was an action you wanted and allowed yourself to become excited about.

We get to use that same type of energy when doing something you are not particularly excited about, in order to eliminate those excuses. The task may not be worthy of excitement, however, if you trick your brain into thinking this will be the best thing ever, and you make the decision to look forward to it, the less those excuses will take over. And the more likely you will be to enjoy it. Two benefits built into one.

Let's take a look at eliminating these beliefs altogether, the most basic way to do this is to address them head on. This is a difficult and even a grueling process, but it must be done for massive growth, so hang in here. Again, sister, you can do hard things – I will continue repeating this, in the case you are not repeating it to yourself. *Bonus, write this down on a paper and put it on your mirror, in your car, on your refrigerator, wherever you know you will see it each day as a reminder.

Take some time now to write down all of your limiting beliefs.

What are the recurring messages you have received about yourself from others – even when you were a child – who did you receive them from? Did/do you believe those messages about yourself? How did those messages make you feel at that time and now?

Where do you feel most stuck in your life right now? What is holding you back? What thoughts do you have about yourself that are holding you back? What is the biggest thing stopping you from being unstuck? What feelings or emotions are brought to the surface when you think about being stuck?

I encourage you to take time, in a quiet place, alone and answer these questions honestly. Do not make anything up, do not leave anything out. You choose who gets to see this information; meaning, not a single soul will if you choose otherwise, so make sure you are being 100% honest with yourself.

Here are some of the most common limiting beliefs – several I have felt and some I still feel myself –

- I am not good enough
- My family won't approve my choices
- I am too scared/fearful
- I don't have what she has
- I don't have the confidence
- I am not worthy
- I lack motivation

You are picking up what I'm putting down? Write down every single thing you believe is limiting you in life.

Let's have a little story time again. My biggest limiting belief while writing this book was no one would want to hear it, no one would read it and I would be judged, heavily. I would be judged for my experience with the twelve steps, my family would not understand why I would choose to put my personal business to the world. I really had to decide whether it was worth it, but here we are. I did believe it, obviously, because if I can help one person, my job is done. If this went out to one person, I could simply be at rest easily. And who cares if I am judged, that is not my focus, my focus is on helping others. And hey, what others think of me is none of my business, so fuck it. Let's go. Let's just start! At the end of this, I know I did my best, followed my heart and was true to myself; that is all that matters here.

We get to be aware and recognize our limitations, in order to push beyond them; in my opinion, it is the only way to move beyond them. If we continue to keep them inside and not acknowledge them, we will continue to let them hold us back. It is time to get vulnerable and honest, even if it is just with yourself. It was time for me, after years of thinking, writing and creating, I finally had to acknowledge what was holding me back in order to move forward. I had to redirect my brain and retrain my focus. But first, I had to recognize the very issues holding me back.

We are what we decide to be. Yes, it is truly possible to just wake up one morning and change. If you wake up one morning and decide you are going to live a fuller, happier life and give yourself the love you deserve, and accept nothing less, that is the moment it becomes possible, when you decide it is possible. When YOU decide. And eliminating our limiting beliefs is a part of that decision, consciously or unconsciously, you are ultimately making the decision to eliminate your life of limiting beliefs the second you decide to change.

You are worthy, motivated, accepted and loved. And now, you get to believe these are true.

Here is the BIG question: do you want to do something about your limited way of thinking, and begin to love yourself fully, as you are? If so, what the fuck are you going to do about it?

Insecurities

We all have these little fuckers, clouding up our brains. They happen to EVERYONE, regardless of size, beauty, and status. Our brains continue to betray us by allowing little thoughts to creep in and keep us from living our full potential. I truly think most insecurities have been implemented on us by insane societal standards, dating back to our grand mama's time.

The brain fears change, so we get to keep working it – like the muscle that it is – to push us to our full life's potential. While we go to the gym to work other muscles, it's time we go to the brain gym and retrain that bad boy. No one can or will do this for you, and no one cares as much about it as you do, it's time to take some actions.

As a friend of mine once said, if you are not tired you are uninspired. Bam! Get inspired, sister!

My biggest insecurity in my entire life was my legs. They are thick, always have been and I never wore shorts, still don't actually. As I got older, I began to discover what that dimply skin was, and was convinced no one else had it. If they made bathing suits that were pants; sister, you better believe I would've owned all the pairs. I hated my legs, hated. My knees always had this dark spot on them which was just weird. They were always dry, no matter the amount of lotion I used. It took me one and half marathon, a ton of workouts, what seemed like endless running and two Spartan races – Spartan races y'all for me to realize they were not changing. No matter how sore they were afterward, no matter how hard I worked or what I did, these thick, dry, cellulite covered legs were here to stay.

A family day at the pool. That's what it took. Not one person looked at my legs funny, not one family member said a word. That's when I realized this insecurity is mine and was in my own head. No one else cared. No one else was poking fun at me. No one else freaking cared, they were happy that I was there with them on a family day. This insecurity was all mine. And dammit, these tree trunks were fucking strong, like incredibly strong and had gotten me through a ton of races, hard times, and helped me walk away from some shitty times, getting me through some freaking Spartan races. They aren't so bad, and I actually really love them. Sure, jeans fit funny and probably always will and I will more than likely always fall into the curvy section of clothing, but who fucking cares?! If I love my legs and know what I have gotten through with them, really, who cares? No one, but me! It's up to me to change my mindset. And I did, and still do from time to time when I see someone with gorgeous feminine legs. It's a work in progress. Own it, own those insecurities and find a way to love them with your whole heart.

Self-Doubts

Self-doubts run along the same lines, limited beliefs and insecurities – self-doubts are too close a cousin to these other delightful traits. It is your brain telling you not to change. Contentment is not a way to live. Contentment, in my experience, will destroy joy and love.

Think back to childhood – what were you told to believe? What were you told you had to do in your life? What were you told about your body, about the way you moved, about the way you dressed? Now, deeply dig about how this has impacted you as an adult. Once you start digging into these thoughts, it will become easier to relate them to actions you are practicing today.

Do you still believe these things to be true?

Do you believe you made some kind of mistakes in your life because you did not follow what other people told you to be true?

Do you look at yourself differently?

Digging into step four:

In this step, we get to sit with ourselves – truly, alone and quiet. We get to think back on all the limiting beliefs we have had in our lives. We get to think of all our insecurities – physical and mental – and write them down, fill up an entire notebook if needed. We get to relive our moments of self-doubt and write those as well.

Without really digging deep on these and writing them out, we will not be capable of moving on, we must confront them head on, to move beyond those limits. I am a strong believer, once you put something down on paper and review it with clear eyes, that is the exact moment you begin to let go.

Take a day, an afternoon or just an hour – sit with yourself, somewhere alone and quiet – and make these lists. I would recommend you take each category and write them out before moving on to the next. Do not leave anything out – you are the only person that will see this list – unless you choose to share it with your trusted person. You are the only one who will take stock of what this means to you. Be honest and open with yourself, which is sometimes one of the hardest things to do; as it is a must to complete this process.

This was so damn difficult for me, and I remember in the midst of going through this one, I heard someone say, how many times have you given up on yourself to watch TV? (I believe that was Miss Rachel Hollis in my brain) That was enough to make me realize the worth of all this; because the answer took innumerable amounts of time. I gave up on myself constantly to sit and watch television. I gave up on goals because Grey's Anatomy was on. I gave up getting some writings done on Sunday because laying in bed and staring at Netflix for six hours sounded so much better. I gave up on doing workout because I had to catch this episode. These examples could go on forever. Do you know how many times I made excuses to get out of my own success?! Do you know how many times I allowed something I was told as a child affect my adult life?! Sister, the list would go on much longer than you would ever want to read.

It wasn't just television; it was so much more than that when I took the time to really think it over. I told myself all the time how bad I was. I couldn't possibly write a book because that was for someone who had it together. No way would anyone want to take advice from me, as I was only good at pretending. How can I give someone tools to make their life better, when I have a marriage that is crumbling? How can I talk to someone about living their dreams, when I consistently give up on my own? How can I show someone how to successfully get their physical body to its healthiest state, when I eat pizza and skip workouts?

The answer was because of those things, that's why. I can tell someone I consistently gave up on myself, but ended up making it happen because it was that important to me. I can tell you how you can make your life more fulfilling because I have been in the position when my life was crumbling, and I made it out alive. I can help someone get their health together because I have been there; I was not perfect, so they don't have to be either. I gave up so much to watch television, but here I am, pushing through and that's what makes me great. I have found the power to use what was not working for me to push me into what has and show others the same way. It is what makes you great as well. We can do hard things, and that is not a joke or an understatement. That is freaking powerful – if you only allow it to be.

You have all the power, and all these things – I mean, these limiting beliefs, insecurities and self-doubts are stepping stones to your greatness. They were in your life for a purpose – to strengthen you to who you need to be, to live your greatest good. Acknowledge them for what they are, and then move forward. This is no little feat, I appreciate that the more you practice and put this into action, the easier it will become to dismiss them the moment they creep into your brain. It takes time, working the muscle and discipline, but imagine the magnitude you could accomplish in your life if you were able to move on from the lies holding you back.

Stop holding back yourself from self-love, happiness and success.

Questions to spark the mind:

- Did I make mistakes? Do they still define me?
- What was I told as a child about myself?
- What was I told I could or could not do?
- What moments in my life do I look at as mistakes? And Why?

Then, ask yourself the ultimate question:

Do I want to change these limiting beliefs, insecurities and self-doubts? Do I see a different way of life for myself?

You are capable of making this change, as you are the only one who is. There is not a soul that can do this for you, no one! You can have support and encouragement but it ends with your actions. No bull shit here, because it cannot live here if you want to progress in life.

Now imagine your life free of all these limiting beliefs, insecurities and self-doubts. Just like all the wonderful things in life, this will not be easy, but it is 100% necessary. Really dig in and day dream for a moment....

What does your life look like without all the junk?

How do you feel?

What are you accomplishing?

Can you see it? Is it not the most beautiful image possible? If it is not, keep going, keep pushing until it is.

Once you have that image in your brain, it will push you to do the work. Every time you have a doubt, a limiting belief, something in your way, stop. Right then, stop. Place that image back in the forefront of your mind and daydream there again. Allow it to consume you until all you can do is push forward harder and faster than you did before. Keep practicing this until all you can see is that bright light of the future begging you to come to it.

These lies will keep you from moving toward your true-self if you let them. If you give them the power, they will hold you back from moving forward. But the kill shot to the lie is the truth. Start showing yourself the truth, every moment you have these feelings, give yourself a truth that will shoot it down immediately.

Project for you: find at least three things you are incredibly good at, no matter what they are. You can be insanely good at mowing the lawn, or being a dog mom, or making your signature dish. It can be as simple as driving, or pumping gas. Whatever those three things are, write them down and stare at them. Anytime you have a self-doubt or a limiting belief, rehearse these to yourself as if your life depended on them – because it does. This is the way to finally kick out those doubts, by giving that lie a truth. Yes, you may not be the best in your industry, but you are killing it at mowing that lawn! You may not be the most excellent public speaker, but dang, you are a superb dog mom. That's all that matters, you ARE good at things, you can accomplish hard things and you matter in the world of others. Once you train your brain to go there, slowly but most definitely surely, those self-doubts, insecurities and limiting beliefs will start to fade into the distant past and you will be unstoppable. You are unstoppable NOW!

I was watching the Rachel Hollis documentary Made for More, and she said she excels in figuring it out. She always figures it out, and I thought, that's me. No matter the situation, I will always find anything out.

So, nothing, really, will stop me, nothing can stand in my way. I will figure it out. Maybe that is you as well, I will venture to guess it is because you are still here. You can do this; you can figure this out. You are unstoppable!

Always kill the lies you experience with the truth; no matter the situation, you will come out stronger and start believing the truth about yourself.

Featured Female – Nikole Glaug

This is ME

Nikole and I met through the social media, mostly because we have several mutual friends through kickball. With sharing her incredible story, I was drawn to her courage, happiness, and free spirit. She pushes through insane workouts that would make most people fall off the wagon, preservers through life challenges, and always has the most amazing smile. She welcomes

people into her life openly and lovingly. I am beyond grateful to have virtually met her and can't wait for the day I can squeeze her in person.

Please, tell us who you are as a human?

I am a 35-year-old trans woman.

What do you do for a living? Why do you choose to do it?

I am an auditor for a bunch of banks, which I chose because it keeps me mentally alert.

Why do you think people lack self-love?

It is simply because we aren't taught or conditioned to self-love.

What are you currently working on that is bring you joy?

Reading more.

When you are at peace, what are you doing? What does that look like?

Relaxing with my cat with a good book next to my big front window.

What does self-love mean to you?

Self-love to me means accepting your flaws and shortcomings, and loving yourself for who you are today. Doing things that bring you joy, and appreciating every day that is given to you.

Do you remember the moment you realized how to love yourself? Will you share that experience?

I don't remember the exact moment, but I try to find one thing to love about myself every day. It could be something as simple as having a good workout, or I did something extraordinarily nice for someone else during the day, or any number of things I do to show myself that I am an amazing person.

What does your support system look like?

Supportive family, and good friends.

Tell me about your journey to love.

My journey to love is still on going. I still have days where I struggle to like myself, let alone love myself. Those are the days I really have to do a lot of positive self-talk and use positive affirmations to turn around a wayward ship.

But my journey has been traditional. I struggled a lot with internal general dysphoria, which is simply my assigned gender at birth not matching my internal or perceived internal gender. This started for me at a very young age and caused me a great deal of turmoil. I didn't understand why I wasn't "normal" like every other boy of my age (this was pre-internet days...yes I am THAT old). I struggled trying to fit in, while I was also being bullied at school.

Those factors added in with gender dysphoria that was undiagnosed led to a severe lack of self-confidence (which is less severe today). My 20's were a time of self-exploration, where I experimented with different ways to be happy; alcohol, drugs, sex and reclusion/exclusion amongst other avenues. None of it worked because I hadn't addressed the core issues that were plaguing me. I had to turn to a few chats/websites/resources that were geared towards people questioning their sexuality and gender around my late 20's and a lot of what I was reading was ringing true to me. These people's coming out stories were such an inspiration for me, which was a super evident that these people loved themselves, their true selves; so immensely that they were willing to put lifelong relationships, education opportunities, jobs and job prospects, housing opportunities, and personal safety on the line. I decided that if I ever

wanted to truly be happy and love myself, that I would need to be honest with myself and my loved ones about who I am as a person. I had some conversations with both my mother and father, which was met with nothing but love and support; including majority of my friends. That alleviated a lot of pressure and stress about what I had been dealing with for such a long time. People would still love me, so it's ok for me to begin to love myself too. So, I started my long journey to learn to love myself, which has not always been easy but worthy. As I sit, 3 years on hormone replacement therapy, I look back at how miserable I was and how much I hated who I was because I was always hiding who I was. Today, I am living my best life, full of love for myself and others, with the hope that the future still holds greater things for me.

What is your single most embarrassing moment?

There are too many to choose from. But one of my most recent embarrassing stories is of the time I completely ripped the back seam of my leggings at the gym doing overhead squats mid workout. My whole entire ass was just out for the whole gym to see, and I still had something like half a workout to complete.

I just took my shirt off, tied it around my waist, finished my workout and then laughed about it with some of the girls in my class.

How did you embrace your self-perceived flaws?

Well, it's a constant struggle to accept my perceived flaws, but I try to look at the flaw as a part of a whole. A flaw is something that can be worked on, a

device made better. If it is something that can't be changed, i.e., being too tall or having shoulders that are too broad, etc., I try to use positive self-talk and change my internal perception of the flaw. I am too tall becomes, I have nice long legs. My shoulders are too broad becomes, my shoulders are powerful, defined and help me well while working out.

You are going to dinner....where do you go and what do you eat?

If I have to go out, I am going to a Mexican restaurant for skinny margaritas and tacos.

Do you believe a higher power is at work in your life? What impact does that have?

I'm not a believer in "God" or anything like that. I believe that there are energies at work with us and that they have an impact on what happens. It's akin to karma, the world gives you what you seek and returns to you the energy you put out into it. Put out positive energy and love, get it in return. Put out negative energy and hate that will find its way back to you as well.

What is your number one piece of advice for women learning to love themselves?

Get off social media, or better yet limit it. If you're on Instagram and start thinking "I'll never look like her" or "I'll never have an ass like that" it's time to delete that negative influence. Find those that inspire you to do better or be better than you were yesterday and pay attention to those things.

How can women connect with you?

Facebook: Nikole Glaug Instagram: Onikole4.

Chapter 5:

Step 5 – Acknowledge to yourself and your person all of these lies.

You may be thinking, Amber, c'mon, I just wrote all these down, what the hell is this acknowledging thing?! And you also may want to skip this step, but please, do not!

You need this moment and this time to truly be real, raw and honest with yourself, and truly acknowledge all of this to yourself, and another person to hold you accountable. Accountability will make all the difference here.

In this step, we get to take the leap with ourselves and honestly have a conversation – yep, talk to yourself – about how those items in step 4 have had an effect on your life.

What was the cause, and how did it impact you?

To be clear, for all the items you listed in step 4, you are going to be the sole cause, because we are directly responsible for every single thing that happens to us – and we get to own that. Yep, everything!

That guy that broke your heart? You are responsible!

The broken toilet downstairs? Yep, that's you!

The shitty situation you are currently in (I hope this isn't the case, but…)? You, again!

Once you take accountability and ownership for everything that happens in your life, you are setting yourself free. I know it seems like the opposite effect, but it is true, you will feel so free when you realize you are solely responsible for your whole life. Nothing is anyone else's fault, and, surprisingly, it is not yours either. I want to acknowledge the difference between fault and responsibility. Fault is blame, and nobody got time for that. Responsibility is mature ownership, and we all got time for that.

You are responsible if you have not been honest with yourself thus far, and therefore, not making progress like you should be. That's on you, excuses are damned.

Whatever the impact, it is all on you. It is also your responsibility to make that change. You are the sole owner of your life, you are the sole changer of the said life. Do not allow this to feel heavy, allow this to feel like the best thing for you, allow it to be the key to building a stronger, more wonderful life for yourself.

My husband, in a profound moment, said to me once; life is going to change, you can either let life dictate that change or you can own the change.

If you are letting life dictate the changes for you, you are giving in to your limiting beliefs, insecurities and self-doubts. When you make the decision to really own the changes, you are in control.

Hold up....

So, now you have taken time to sit with yourself, to review all of those limiting beliefs, insecurities and self-doubts. Now you get to ask the question: Am I really ready to let go? Am I ready to control my life and take responsibility for all that happens to me and for me?

If the answer is no, it's ok. It is hard to let go of these things, they have been with us for a very long time. They have allowed us to feel comfortable, they have been our excuses not to move on from tough situations. They have kept us from doing big, giant, and heart leaping things. They have been our soft place to fall when things got heavy. They have kept us by fearing something new. When we do something over and over our entire lives, it is all we know, and therefore, may take some time to get it together and move on.

It's cool, I get it. But you don't get to move on yet. You get to stay here, in step 5 – and maybe a little in step 4 – and really get to the bottom of these little fuckers.

If that is where you are, own it. It is your responsibility to move forward, no excuses. You cannot properly do that until you can acknowledge and own everything. You cannot do that until you have confronted your limiting beliefs and told them to fuck off. Until you have written down all your insecurities and kicked them to curb. Until you have pumped yourself up so high that self-doubt is no longer in your brain. You get to own this. You get to meet yourself where you are. And it's alright, this expedition is going to look different for every single person. Stay in your lane, put your blinders on, and focus on your own progress.

And please, get this now, even when you have made the decision to change, it does not magically happen. You do not go to bed one night and magically wake up, pour yourself a cup of coffee, and say yep, I fucking owned those ass holes, I am good to go. You may wake up and make the decision which is the foundation, then the work comes in.

It is a muscle and it will have to be worked on every day, for the rest of your life. There you will be, happy and ready to command that you no longer have these shits around, and BAM! You set a goal and that voice creeps back in to say you can't do that, why are you even trying. That's when you work it!!! That's when you make the conscious decision to say no to that voice. To scream at it, SHUT UP! It doesn't happen overnight, and it is an everyday work.

Let me just tell you how quickly my decision came for this book, and how confident I felt in that decision, I had nothing in my brain telling me not to do it. Yea…right. The decision came clear as day, and landed me smack dap on my computer typing away at the keys like a bird in the park pecking at the seed. However, this process and my brain did not mesh well together. I had several doubts coming in, several lies telling me no one would even read this, it would never be good enough, that I am in no way to compete with professional writers. The decision came easy, but the process was not easy. I had to work and push through all those thoughts and lies. I had to continuously kill the lies with truths about myself and I just had to keep writing. I told myself, I would just write and not publish anything. So. Many. Doubts.

This was all AFTER I put in so much work on myself. This was after I went through this process, this was after I thought I eliminated all of those lies. I did the work dammit, and there I was allowing these lies to creep back in and hold me back from my truth. I was brain dumped, I cried, I yelled, I had meetings with myself and my person, I did it all and here I am. I felt like I was back at square one. But that is the lie I was telling myself. I was not at square one, but no one is immune, even after you put in all the work. You have to continue the work, or your brain will revert to your previous habits. It took you years to tell yourself all those lies; I am in the mind to think it will take twice as long to break them.

No one is immune, keep putting in the work.

Taking Control...

Finally, it's about damn time. You are taking your life in your own hands. How freaking powerful is that?!

So, now is the hard part. Remember that person in step 3, that person you trusted that fully supports you. You need to have a conversation with that person.

It might be super hard, and it might just be super easy, you get to decide which. In order to truly get to work on yourself, I cannot say this enough, you get to have accountability with what you are accomplishing. Else, there is not a standard to hold yourself to.

Sit down with this person, or tribe of people, and go over your list – as much or as little as you prefer. Yes, I know, I said no one would see this list but you, and that is the truth, only you will see the list, it is up to you how much you share; though, the more you share, the more you will grow – another reason I stress your person must be trustworthy to you.

Here's the important part. You get to preface this conversation. Explain to your person what you are trying to accomplish with this homework and allow them to be aware of the growth you are achieving with this. Also, they are there to listen, you get someone to listen and then call you on your bull shit. If they notice any of these behaviors in you, they get to call you on it, and you don't get to be mad with them, either. I'll take this moment to say, get over yourself.

That is one of the reasons this relationship gets to be chosen carefully. And it must be raw and honest for it to work. If it is not, take responsibility for choosing the wrong person and go back on the hunt.

I would recommend you check in with this person once per week, depending on your needs, it may be more often. Let them know where you are and what you need from them, or what you will need from them going forward. Have a clear-cut direction for the conversation, so you do not leave anything out or get side tracked.

If you find yourself in conflict with the person you chose, that is ok, we are changing and growing, and we get to have someone adapt to those changes and growth. If you need to find a new person, again, go back on the hunt. The right person for this is there for you to find.

Now, you have taken control and have someone to keep you on track with that control. Again, allow that relationship to remain open, honest and trustworthy.

Some questions to reflect on:

- How have I been completely honest with this reflection?
- How am I practicing being open to a new way of thinking?
- What actions am I taking to have full responsibility for my own life?
- Why have I chosen the person I have? What qualities

do they possess that I value?
- How have I chosen to move forward?

Ideas on how to talk to your person:

First, explain what you are doing and what you hope to accomplish here. Explain what you would like their role to be with you and how often you would like to check in. If they agree to the check-ins, have an agenda and a time expectation, so there are no lingering conversations or taking up too much of your time or theirs.

I would also suggest offering them something in return. You could be the same for them, or offer to brainstorm ideas, make this a team effort and therefore not solely about you and your expedition. Both of you will feel more fulfilled and grateful for it in the end.

Allow them the comfort to give you tough love and let you know when you are acting in ways of the past, be clear that you will not be offended; then, do not get offended if they give you unpleasant feedbacks. This has to be a two-way street and both of you have to be honest, as you get to practice taking in constructive criticism, so you are able to grow and notice where you need to work.

Finally, allow this to be fun. That is what this is all about. It is work, and it will be grueling at some points, but it should always be fun for you to learn more about yourself and grow into the person you were meant to be all along. Let it be empowering that you are taking control and gaining a new perspective on life.

Chapter 6:

Step – Now you have revealed a lot about yourself, are you ready to make a real change?

Steps 4 and 5 are a bit rough but necessary for a real change. Now that you have taken stock of your limited beliefs, insecurities and self-doubts – have you told someone or a group you trusted completely? – it is time to decide to truly make a change in yourself.

This decision to make the change comes somewhat easily, we can easily say we want a change, it is our actions that matter most here. We are about to embark on a true expedition and if done properly – meaning, for yourself and no one else – it will be the greatest expedition of your life. You will wake up to your own life, and the magic will inevitably start happening.

Meditation

It is time to wholly and completely change your mindset. For this, I recommend adding in some sort of mediations to your life. This is a practice, so you get to keep working on it. Over time, and with work, meditation changes your composure, your mind and your confidence.

The misconception is that meditation is sitting for a long period of time with the outcome being a thoughtless, clear mind. This is false! Just by doing a quick search, you will find meditations lasting only 5 minutes, if you don't have five minutes for yourself, you don't have a life. Feel me?

There are meditations you can incorporate while driving or doing laundry or making dinner. There are meditations that require you to sit or lie still and close your eyes. This practice is one of convenience, and so long as you make the time to focus, it will work to your best benefit.

There are groups in all areas with all types of people you could sign up and try out. You may just love the class, get some clarity and meet some amazing new people. Sounds like something everyone should be doing in their lives, don't you think?

There are also common mistakes with meditation. This is a process of allowing your mind to wander, but always bringing it back in. You are not looking for a completely clear mind, just realizing when your thoughts wander and bringing them back to the breath. That's truly meditation, and it does take practice. Eventually, you will get to the point of pure mindfulness completely clearing your mind, but do not start thinking that is the purpose. Start with five minutes' guide on YouTube, or grab the app Headspace for free and get some practices done and see how you feel.

Some of my favorites are by the master mindfulness mentor, Jon Kabat Zinn. You will not regret looking him up and taking on some guided meditations, bonus that his voice is incredibly soothing. Like I stated before, grab up the app Headspace, it is free and meditations are ten minutes or less, which is a great place to get started. Ask a friend, or post on Facebook, I am sure you know several people who meditate and practice mindfulness that would be willing to help you out. If all else fails, simply hit the search bar and find a local place to go.

Mindfulness

This leads me on to mindfulness. I have done extensive research in this area and with tons of practices, I've come to realize that mindfulness makes life so much fuller.

Mindfulness is the practice of truly living your life moment by moment, in the moment, and for the moment. No, I am not saying to forget about goals for the future, but each moment, attempt to live it fully in the present. Always plan for the future, however, think about what you can do in this moment to get where you need to be.

Again, do not let this be intimidating or allow it to escape your to do list, this gets to be something you practice throughout the day, not something you write down and check off. It is simply noticing when you are not living in the moment, and when you think you are failing, know you are right where you need to be. I feel like I am failing with this, every single day; however, realizing that and going back to the moment actually means I am successful here. This is the one practice where feeling like failing is a success, because you are recognizing it and correcting it. Pretty cool!

Examples of mindfulness in simplicity are when you are walking, feel your feet pressing against and leaving the pavement. Notice the colors and smells around you – unless you are near a dumpster, that may not make your life full. My favorite example is when you are in the shower, check and make sure you are in the shower (thanks Jon Kabat Zinn!). Most of my thoughts come to me in the shower, and I hear this a lot, but I have noticed, I don't take in the moment, I don't feel the water hitting my body, notice the smells of my body wash and shampoo or the soothing sounds of the water. When you are eating, notice the tastes of the food, the feeling as you chew, the fullness entering your body – this may also start to make you appreciate foods that heal your body. This is mindfulness, and it will allow you to be more present in your life; therefore, live life fully and also be more present with others, making your relationships better as well.

Like meditation, this is also a practice, and it takes time and effort to be fully aware. It will not just come to you one day and stay forever, it takes some building of the mindful muscle.

We have all heard the phrase, "stop and smell the roses," and this is literally in the sense of mindfulness, really smell those roses, take it all in and enjoy it in that moment.

Making a Change

This is a full-on commitment. You will not accomplish self-love in a day, and it will not stay in your life without work – much as I wish, that was not the case.

Let's reflect on this:

What is your idea of self-love?

What can you do to better love you, the way you are now?

I hear it all the time. Once I have a better job, I will be happier. Once I lose this weight, I will be more joyful and happier with the way I look. Once I have more money in the bank and buy that house and get my dream car, I will be fulfilled.

The bad news, my friends, not one of these things will make you happier. Read this carefully: Nothing external in this world will make you a happier human. Nothing! It is internal and all your choice, your responsibility to live a full life.

If you are not currently happy with yourself - a new job, car, house, more money or less weight on your bones will not make you happier with yourself. And while we are here, it is totally unfair to place that burden on another person. Nothing they do can or will actually make you happy.

Well, we are here, so let's talk about it. Relationships are a tricky game. And though, this is all about a relationship with yourself, so often it is said that "he/she is making me so mad," "he/she should know how to make me happy." I am sounding out the bull shit horn loud and clear, so you hear it no matter where you are.

Loud and clear. No external relationship will make you happy. Not a single one! They can make you feel good, feel attractive, fulfilled…. but never happy. I am also going to sound the old truth, if you are not happy with you, nothing else is going to change that. And honestly, you are going to sabotage every other relationship in your life because you are unhappy, nothing they do is going to change your mindset, which causes arguments because they are not living up to what YOU cannot do for yourself. See how unfair that is?! And this is not specific to romantic relationships. I have definitely sabotaged some friendships for these very reasons.

I have had friendships crumble because they were bettering themselves and I was jealous, or someone I felt was prettier/smarter/you name the trait, and I felt the need to put them down thinking that would make me feel better. Sure, it did not! I had relationships I criticized to death because I was unhappy with ME, there was nothing they could do, no matter what they changed, I was also unhappy with them because of myself. This does not limit to one type of relationship in your life, it will happen everywhere, even with parents – maybe especially with parents, sorry mom and dad – if you do not get a hold of yourself, look in the mirror and do some works. I have been there, and sometimes I am still there, as I have to do the work all over again.

However, the cool part here is if you are in a relationship and unhappy with yourself, you can absolutely stay in that relationship while working on you. Hell, I was married when I started this expedition. He had nothing to do with it, it was about me. Relationship status has nothing to do with this. You can work on yourself whether you are in a great relationship or single and ready to mingle. But I promise you this, the more you work on your own self-love, the more you will watch your relationships dramatically change for the better.

The connections with your family and friends will also change in this expedition. You will notice some people slowly drifting away – they are not ready for you to change – and notice some drawing in more closely to you – they are truly happy for you and ready to see you make changes, not only for yourself but also to better their own relationship with you.

Let's talk about the drifters, some relationships will drift, and that is perfectly fine. Some people like the way you are now, and do not want to see any change in you. They do not want to change themselves and therefore, if anything changes around them, they are resistant to it. Let them go! It is for YOUR own good and that is what we are working on here. They may see a difference in you and that may inspire them to change themselves. But, they may just talk that ish and walk away, and you need them to. You may not see it this way in the beginning, but they are actually doing you a huge favor. It is dramatic what good this can do for your life. The negativity drops away and you stop stressing about having a connection with someone who doesn't want to see the true you. It is going to hurt, and it will be difficult, but the more love you show yourself, the stronger you will be against this resistance, and the easier it will be to distance from these relationships.

The great part…those who love you will see the changes and be your biggest cheerleader. They will start to draw closer to you, look up to you and inspired themselves. These are your people. And the interesting part is you will start to realize the ones that are drawn into you are the ones also working on living their lives fully and happily. You will be perfectly aligned with the perfect people for you.

The happier and open you are with yourself, the more everything around you changes, including your relationships.

Now, back to you. Are we clear on the fact that nothing external will help you in this process? That we need to make this about us, for us and by us?

Repeat this phrase: I am learning to love myself, for myself and by myself. Each day, I will work to make progress. Other people have no responsibility here, and it is unfair to give it to them. Other people's judgements of my expedition hold no bearing for me.

Have you ever flown on a plane? If not, go somewhere, like now.

If so, you know the safety demonstration – it is not used in a ton of personal development because of how perfect of an explanation it is; put your own oxygen mask on first before helping anyone else, including children. Because guess what…if you don't and you lose consciousness, you are of no help to anyone, including yourself.

That is what this expedition is all about. Putting on your own oxygen first. Pouring into your own cup first. Having an overflowing pitcher, whatever metaphor you find most helpful.

You are your number one priority. Now, I know this is hard to swallow, especially if you are a woman, and even more so if you are a mother. No offense guys or dads. But women have a built-in guilt factor and this is horsefuckery. We are constantly trying to take care of everyone else. Enough!

You get to take care of everyone else, of course. But only after you have taken care of yourself, whatever that means to you. You are now required to put on your own oxygen mask before you help anyone put on theirs. If you are neglecting yourself, you are not being a good person, a good friend, significant other, mother/father, or family member. You are just not. You are not being good to others by allowing yourself to fall out of love with you.

Think back to when you were a child. You did not care what anyone else thought, and you were the number one priority. You did not care if mom and dad could afford it, or if they were ready to leave or if they hadn't prepared to make dinner. When you were ready, you were ready and that was it. If you needed a nap, you probably took one. Let's bring back our inner child. Start thinking that way, if you need something, it needs to be met first. That way, you can better take care of others. And while we are there, let's bring back taking naps, sister. Adults need them too.

We have to let go of what others think of us. This will be a common conversation as we go through each step, because it is so important.

Why do we always care so much about what other people think of us? Try to take some time to reflect on that and come up with an honest answer for yourself. Once we let go of this, life really begins to open up because we start to make decisions based on our wants and needs, instead of what others want for our lives. It is the most freeing feeling on the planet, I am fairly certain.

You are now required to put yourself first, and you are also required to stop thinking of that as being selfish. Where that thought came from is beyond me, this process is anything but not selfish. Imagine what the world would look like if we all showed up as our true selves, full of love for ourselves and happy.

I guarantee fighting over the last DVD on sale on black Friday would never happen again. Getting pissed at the guy who took the last cart at the grocery store wouldn't happen. Getting impatient over a customer taking forever in line. We would all be looking more for the happiness in any situation, and probably be more talkative with one another, getting to know the other people, while waiting in those long lines instead of being impatient and pissed. Imagine a world like that.

Now, I want you to think what your life looks like putting yourself first. What would you do to take care of yourself? How will your attitude change toward yourself and others? How would you help other people? How would your relationships change?

I ask you to reflect on these questions, so that you are focused on what life would look like. This will keep you on track with your self-love. When you continue to remind yourself what life looks like when you are loving yourself, you will continue to push to get there.

And I am in the trenches doing this with you. Every now and then, I revert to my old impatient, angry self, especially for some reasons during grocery shopping. While we are here, let's have a public service announcement: be freaking patient at the grocery store and please be aware other people are also at that grocery store. Thanks. And I still have to bust this out and remind myself that I get to practice patience today, I get to remind myself to be in the moment, with the love and gratitude I have in my life. This shit keeps me sane and is necessary. But all of that goes to show, I am in this with you and it takes time, and even then, you will still need reminders. But the fact you are reminding yourself is huge, you are growing so much in those moments.

Once you have made the decision and commitment to change, it is on to step 7 to continue this awesome expedition.

Reflection questions:

- Can I let go of other people's thoughts of me? What does that feel like?
- Can I truly let go of my negative thoughts of myself? How will I do that?
- Can I practice this each day and work on my self-love muscle?
- Am I willing to dig deep with this program and change my life?

Featured Female – Amanda Moyle

This is ME

Mandy and I were in a virtual fitness group together initially. We finally met in person in New Orleans for a conference, and I loved her sunny outlook and how excited she was just to meet people. Her excitement was

contagious. Thankfully, with social media, we have kept in contact, and I have watched her growth over the years, and I am so honored she decided to jump and get interviewed.

Who are you as a human?

Just a small town girl hustling for herself to fulfill her dreams!

What do you do for a living? Why do you choose it?

Entrepreneur, because I finally reached a point where I could see that my bosses didn't truly care about my success. I have learned more about myself in the past year as an entrepreneur than in the last twelve years working for someone else.

Why do you think people lack self-love?

Many people are never taught that it's a necessary part of life. I know for me, my mom wasn't taught much self-love and she didn't know how to show me to do the same. We are taught at a young age that we should do for others, but we need to be taught that we need to always come first before someone else's needs or desires.

What are you currently working on that is bringing you joy?

Building two businesses, one for my creative DIY passion and other is a home based travel agent. It's always been something I wanted to do, but I let others talk me out of it twelve years ago. No more!

When you are at peace, what are you doing? What does that look like?

Sitting in my cozy apartment with Christmas lights on, watching TV with my fiancé while our three cats sleep peacefully.

What does self-love mean to you?

Being able to truly see my worth by not asking people's opinions anymore. It's all I've ever known and recently realized I'd never made a decision that was fully my own. That I had ALWAYS considered or asked someone's opinion before, and it truly just broke my heart. We get to stand in our power and realize how incredible we are. Doing anything that helps you reassure yourself of how important you are, is self-worth in my eyes.

Why do you think self-love is important?

I believe we cannot live our best life without knowing what self-love is or how to perform it. It truly starts at our core, and once the inside is healing, we can work on the outside and any other aspects of life that have struggled because of the cracks in the foundation.

Do you remember the moment you realized how to love yourself? Will you share that experience?

I don't know that it was one moment. It's been a series of moments ever since I dove into the world of personal development in 2015. The idea that there's an entire world I haven't mentally experienced yet was astounding to me. That beyond the dark and dysfunctional chaos I had grown up; I could literally create the shining beacon of light I had been searching for my entire life. It's been an amazing journey, and every step I take reminds me that I'm right where I always need to be, whether it's hard or not.

What does your support system look like?

My main support system is my fiancé, Matt, and my best friend Sarah. I have a ton of good friends all over, and now I have a Mentorship filled with incredible women to support me. My family supports me but typically only if it's what they want me to do. If it's not, they aren't sure how to and in turn criticize the unknown. I've had to set my own boundaries from toxic relationships and learn how to protect my energy.

Tell me about your journey to love.

I have seen love with a very different perspective growing up in a very broken and dysfunctional family. The words I love you didn't always feel genuine, and sometimes, had strings attached. Love is meant to be shown, the actual word doesn't mean much to me. It's more important that someone takes the genuine effort to express their love however it's best for you to receive it properly. That could look a million different ways for a million different people.

What is your single most embarrassing moment?

I honestly can't think of anything specific, I'm always doing weird and awkward things in public that most people would think was embarrassing, but it doesn't bother me. Life is meant to be fun, and I try to never take anything too seriously.

How did you embrace your self-perceived flaws?

By realizing that they are mine, nobody else can have them. They are unique parts of who I am, and I deserve to own that part of my personality.

You are going to dinner…where do you go and what do you eat?

Mexican hands down…tacos, chips and salsa, margarita.

Do you believe a higher power is at work in your life? What impact does that have?

Maybe? I wasn't raised religiously, but I tend to call myself spiritual. I believe the universe has its plan somewhat laid out, and it's up to us to make our choices as we see fit, and deal with the kickback if it turned out to be a lesson we needed to learn.

What is your number one piece of advice for women learning to love themselves?

Stop asking everyone's opinions. Ask yourself first, stand in your decision. Else, others will give their opinions without you asking for them.

How can women connect with you?

Email: Mandy73188@yahoo.com

Facebook: facebook.com/mandy7318806

Featured Female – Jami Pham

This is ME

I firmly believe the universe has plans for certain people to come together no matter what, and this is true for Jami and I. Yet another amazing soul I met online and completely fell in love with. We roomed together at a conference

and I just knew it was meant to be. She is one of the kindest souls I have ever met and love to talk with, while she would also listen to you like it was her job. She is a wife and an incredible artist.

Who are you as a human?

I am an artist and a teacher by nature, but not necessarily by profession. I feel value when I can be a resource to someone. You may say I have a servant's heart. I'm happiest when I'm in the kitchen cooking for my loved one, especially my husband. But if I feel like you expect me to do any of the above, my rebel soul will come to play. I am very mothering, but not quite a mother. Except for my fluffy creatures. They love me unconditionally, and I'm blessed every day they chose to stick around. I am an early riser who appreciates the morning quiet and a hot cup of coffee after yoga. I'm quite the conundrum and I think I like it that way.

What do you do for a living? Why do you choose it?

I'm an insurance professional. I have a background in claims, which I hated every second of, and I have recently switched to retirement financial products. I don't necessarily have a burning passion for the role I'm in, but I do believe in utilizing all resources you have to grow your dream. Right now, that looks like helping to build someone else's dream (and get the big corporate perks) while building a side hustle and my dream on the side. It's the best of both worlds.

#hannahmontana

Why do you think people lack self-love?

We live in a society that respects the martyrs. Work hard, never sleep and work just to pay your bills and die. I really think people believe this. I've lost self-love in the past because I didn't feel worthy of it. I barely felt worthy of the outside world's attention at various points in my life, why would I love myself if no one else does? It's a sad reality but it's true, we place so much value on the outside opinion we don't know what we even like to do ourselves sometimes. How can we create a friendship with ourselves if we don't even know who we are?

What are you currently working on that is bringing you joy?

Meal planning workshop turning into an online academy...podcast with a childhood bestie... Magical Mentorship 2019!

When you are at peace what are you doing? What does that look like?

Creating anything! Getting my hands dirty and proving to myself I am capable.

What does self-love mean to you?

A relationship with myself that I choose to honor my wishes, but I hold myself accountable to what is for the greater good. Who is better to start with than yourself if you wish to be the change?

Do you remember the moment you realized how to love yourself? Will you share that experience?

It's still a work in progress but I feel glimmers if radiant pride in myself when I can quickly answer with a boundary setting response. I've been so quick to be a people pleaser in my past but being able to say I need to think about something or just a quick no thanks has been everything when it comes to loving myself.

What does your support system look like?

My husband and my online coaching team.

Tell me about your journey to love.

It's still going but every time I choose me I feel empowered. I fall back, but I ask my support system to be there when they see me slipping.

What is your single most embarrassing moment?

Failing at a job I thought I would be good at and turned out I was not.

How did you embrace your self-perceived flaws?

This has taken a lot of inner works and journaling. If I'm able to bring voice to something it doesn't carry as much shame. It helped me to talk about it with myself and a counselor.

You are going to dinner…where do you go and what do you eat?

Anything Mexican!!! Chips and Salsa are a must and of course, I'll pay extra for the guacamole! I'll probably also order a few street tacos.

Do you believe a higher power is at work in your life? What impact does that have?

The universe is all one huge energy, and it plays on the power you put out into the world. I've watched it happen when I'm cognizant of it and I've reflected on past situations and saw it played out after. Either way, the universe is a powerful force in my life for the energy I choose to put out there.

What is your number one piece of advice for women learning to love themselves?

Surrender. Just pick something that feels right for you and trusts the process.

How can women connect with you?

Facebook: Jami Pham

Instagram: @x3jamilee

Chapter 7:

Step 7 – Are you ready to step into a new mindset and way of Life?

Somewhere along the way, someone is going to tell you that you don't have what it takes, that you cannot accomplish true self-love and happiness. You may hear some passive aggressive comments like, oh that's great, I could never do that though, I love my family. Please, refrain from cursing these people – or defending yourself.

Somewhere along the way, someone is going to tell you how incredible they think you are and how you inspired them to make some changes as well.

Somewhere along the line, you will stop worrying. Here is what I have found – for every one person that is not supportive, or talks you down, there are at least two who are your biggest fucking cheerleaders. Either way, you will stop worrying about other people's opinions about what you are doing, as well, you will stop worrying about whether someone thinks your expedition is incredible or incredibly stupid. It won't matter anymore, because you will have realized this is solely about you.

That is when step 7 comes in to play. When you are truly ready to take on a new way of life. When you are committed to making the decision to change.

This moment happened for me when I realized I have been living with Amber my whole life, and I started to really love our relationship. I realized I have a profound friend in her, and I wanted that to continue. This is the freaking moment, friends. This is when the magic truly happens, and you get to come alive in that moment.

I had this moment after doing a ton of research, reading and speaking with others about love. I had done the work and I was developing a system for myself but nothing was happening. I was not fully in it and committed, but something clicked when I looked in the mirror and was yet again unhappy with my weight, my skin and the way my hair fell. I looked right at myself and I said, Amber, this is fucking enough! What are you doing to yourself?! This skin is yours and it is not going to get any better if you keep bitching about it. This weight is on you because you have turned to food over and over instead of just dealing with, your issues and you keep giving up on taking care of yourself. Your hair is pretty gorgeous, and you just get to learn how to style it better, so you feel good about yourself – oh yea, and freaking wash it more than twice a week. To better explain, I read somewhere that celebrities only wash their hair twice a week, I am pretty sure they are leading consumers of dry shampoo and use at least two bottles per week to supplement the lack of hair washing.

It clicked when I realized how hard I was being on myself, and instead of changing my mindset to shift my thinking to something that served me better, I just kept being an ass hole to myself, which made me felt awful, which definitely did not make me want to improve, and the carousel goes round and round again. I wasn't improving because I literally hated every ounce of myself. I was unhappy because instead of seeing what was amazing about myself, and how much my body had endured up to that point, I just kept being negative about myself. Instead of speaking positivity in my being, I just kept making things worse by being my own worst enemy, instead of my own best friend. And this still happens, even with all this practice loving me, I still have to check myself when I make a comment to me about myself. It's not easy, but it has been worth the effort I had invested.

Your beliefs about you will determine your feelings, thoughts, behaviors in all areas of life. Once you make the decision for change and are committed to it, your beliefs about yourself take a jump start to love. You choose love over fear in every situation and push past the limits. And I will be the first to tell you, once this happens, you automatically start taking better care of yourself because you want to. Not because society or someone else told you to, but you really feel it's true to you to take care of yourself in a way you never knew before. Spiritually, mentally, physically and emotionally.

I want to make this clear: You get to change your beliefs about yourself at any time. That is the beauty in this. It is all in your hands. It is your choice and responsibility. This is because you were one way most of your life, and that does not mean you have to stay there, you get to change whenever and however you feel will be the truest to you. Truly such a beautiful expedition.

So, how to make the choice and practice it every day?

Create a dialog with yourself. No more fucking around with this.

Journal it out.

Take ten minutes out of each day and journal about your day. What are you noticing about yourself? What changes have you consciously made and what impact has that had on your mindset? What pissed you off and how did you handle it? What setbacks did you experience? Writing about your setbacks, in my opinion, is super important to move past them. Discuss how you were more mindful in your moments and how that made you feel. When in doubt, write it out.

As a side note, and because I am obsessed with notebooks, I suggest getting a super pretty notebook and a nice pen to make this happen. It helped me, and I may be slightly nuts in the notebook department, but it may help you as well.

Find a ritual

A ritual is something you will do with yourself, for yourself every day. Don't let it be intimidating or daunting. Maybe it will be waking up in the morning and saying out loud what you are grateful for. Or posting on social media something that makes you happy. Maybe it's taking a few minutes before getting out of bed each morning to just breathe intentionally. It could be getting a workout in before you start your day. Or taking a walk and breathing in the smells and taking in the sights of the morning. Maybe it is cooking something you love for dinner each night and eating with pleasure. Or taking a few moments in the morning to sip coffee and sit outside to start the day right. Even taking time in the morning to plan out your day so you are less stressed, can make an impact on your self-love. Rituals are an easy way to start a life changing habit.

Post it up

Hear me out on this one before you pass by it. Write yourself a message and tape it to your mirror or post it up on the fridge, somewhere you will see it every day, to remind you of your expedition. Let it be a love note to yourself. Something good about you to ensure when you see it, it will remind you how much you love yourself. I am a firm believer in the power of visual ques. If you see something every day, it will remind you what you are doing and where you are headed and is insanely powerful. Take a moment and read it to think about it. It could be as simple as "I am Enough" post it on your mirror, so you see it in the morning while brushing your teeth. This is a simple work, and it doesn't have to be hard. Some suggestions: I am enough, I am working on myself each day, I am better than I was yesterday, I am loved, I am powerful. You get the idea. Bonus, if you take a photo for social media and hashtag #DYEPostItUp

Meditation and Mindfulness

We have gone over these two powerful tools – probably the two most powerful in your toolbox. Take time to do a little meditation, even if it is just sitting in silence for five minutes each day, to reflect and clear your brain. I once heard that twenty minutes of meditation is equal to four hours of sleep. How crazy awesome is that?! How refreshed could you feel! I highly encourage you to take on this practice, even if only a few times to see how you feel. Also, learning about mindfulness and making the attempt to work harder at being mindful. Stop and smell those freaking roses.

Write a letter to yourself

Can you tell I am a fan of writing things out? There is a certain power in writing to yourself. You get to fully express how you feel, how far you have come, your setbacks, your improvements, all without anyone else having input. There is a great website, futureme.org, and you can actually write an email to your future self and schedule when it will be sent to you. I have done this several times and forgot I did it, so a year later I get a surprise email from myself and get to read about where I was at that point and really reflect on how far I have come. There is freedom in being real, raw and honest, especially with yourself. I wrote one with the start of a new job or a big life change – definitely wrote one out when I got married, and a year later there it was in my inbox. It is incredible to see how far you have come in certain areas of life, or how ideas have evolved over time.

Talk it out

Schedule a phone call or a coffee date with your person, or someone in your tribe. Talk out where your setbacks are and craft a plan to correct what needs to be corrected. Talk about how far you have come and verbalized how you are feeling. This can make a dramatic difference in the way you view your expedition. Ask the person to just listen and only add input if you ask them. Their job is to be your sounding guide, to listen and provide you with feedback only when necessary. Have a plan ready to go on how you are going to move forward and ask if they heard anything in your conversation that may need adjustment. Having someone on this ride with you is the ultimate tool in keeping you going, staying motivated and calling out your bull shit.

Take Massive Action

Decide to commit and you will succeed. When you finally make the decision, it is time to take massive action. It is time to start taking each moment by the balls and making sure it is serving you with what you need in life. I want you to ask yourself in all situations, will it bring me joy? Is it helpful for my life's vision? If not, really evaluate if it is necessary in your life. And here's a hard truth, even a family event may not be necessary in your life – I have had to decline several while writing this book because they were not aligned with my visions and goals, hard as it may have been, it was worth saying no. And if the answer is yes, DO IT! With your whole heart. Taking massive action will allow you to face fears and break away from the comfy old comfort zone, this is necessary for growth. You may have setbacks, and that is alright, start where you are and build back up. You may have moments you want to say yes and once in the moment, realize the answer should have been no. Just adjust as you go, over time, you will know the difference between what you need and what you don't. If your immediate reaction is no, go with it. Don't worry about hurting feelings – remember, some people just will not understand.

Once you start loving yourself, you will automatically start surrounding yourself with good. You will just start to immerse yourself in everything that brings you joy, and people that support you and uplift you and your expedition. You will start to stray away from the negative – including our own attitude – and distance yourself from situations and individuals that bring you down. It will happen, you just have to take massive action and jump into the self-love expedition. It does take time, but it will start happening before you even realize it is.

Reflection questions:

- How can I create a life of reminders for my expedition?
- What brings me joy?
- How can I practice immersing myself in joy?
- How can I remind myself of my love for myself?
- What rituals do I get to start for myself?
- How can I be more mindful in my life?
- What can I do for myself each day?

Featured Female – Cassie David

This is ME

I first met Cassie years ago because I was dating her brother, the universe truly works in awesome ways. I was always so nervous around her, but she is so warm and welcoming, that no one needs to be. She just left her full time job to chase her dreams, helping others with their health and fitness and has some amazing Instagram content! Her passion for health shines through everything she does, as you can feel her heart in her posts.

Who are you as a human?

I'm one of those introverted extroverts! I feel deeply. I'm loyal and honest. I love being alone and at the same time love a good party. I'm passionate, driven and determined to reach my goals.

What do you do for a living? Why do you choose to do that for a living?

Health coaching.

Why do you think people lack self-love?

I think it's a lack of understanding of how important it is.

What are you currently working on that is bringing you joy?

Building my business! My last day of work was yesterday with a company I've been with for 8 years; now, I'm into health coaching and building my brand.

When you are at peace, what are you doing? What does that look like?

Happy, content, no rush to do anything and no obligations.

What does self-love mean to you?

It means filling your own cup first. Loving yourself so you can love others.

Why do you think self-love is important?

The way you treat yourself sets the tone for how you treat others.

Do you remember the moment you realized how to love yourself? Will you share that experience?

I recognized how I felt. I was burnt out form corporate job. Very overwhelmed and anxious and in desperate need of a break. On a Monday that I was feeling very overwhelmed, I then found out my grandmother had died. I didn't know how I would make it through the week, as I was so broken. I took 5 days off work to grieve and take care of myself, and that saved me. The 5 days of stillness, self-love, self-care, patience, and just being present in the moment completely reset me before I went back to work on Monday. I was a new woman!

What does your support system look like?

Friends, family, and mentors

Tell me about your journey to love.

You have to love yourself first before you can love others. It takes patience and time, but it's important to do your acts of self-love – it's also enjoyable.

What is your single most embarrassing moment?

I truly can't think of one.

How did you embrace your self-perceived flaws?

I remember that they are just differences. My flaw doesn't mean anything. It is no different than one person being blonde and the other being brunette, it's just a different hair color. The way I am is different from the next person.

Rather than viewing it as flaws (negative connotation), it's just differences.

You are going to dinner, where do you go and what do you eat?

Sushi bar!

Do you believe a higher power is at work in your life? What impact does that have?

Yes – I believe that you get what you put out there.

What is your number one piece of advice for women learning to love themselves?

Know your worth!

How can women connect with you?

Email: cassiedavid89@gmail.com

Facebook: Cassie David Instagram: @cassiedavidfit

Chapter 8:

Step 8: Forgive and apologize for not being good to yourself.

Forgiveness is the final form of love. ~Reinhold Niebuhr

This is the time we get to be real with ourselves and learn how to forgive. Again, this will not be a quick and effortless process, none of this is, are you catching on to that?

We get to forgive all our past mistakes, the time we didn't put ourselves first, the days we thought were bad, everything.

What I suggest for this step is putting pen to paper. Take some time and think over everything you beat yourself for. Not getting into that school, not making health a priority, sleeping with that one guy (or guys, I don't judge) and not because you loved him, being a bitch to your parents, cussing out your neighbor – I may or may not have been in all these places with you.

We get to go over every single thing we look back on and regret, or get upset over, or just feel silly about. You get to take stock of every moment you didn't feel true to yourself. And write it down, I truly believe there is real power in putting pen to paper and allowing thoughts to release from your brain.

I say this in the most loving way possible, don't be a little bitch about this. Don't lie to yourself. You get to take time to go back through these moments, but this is a process to heal, not to have a pity party for yourself. If you feel yourself going back to those moments too in depth, snap out of that shit and get to work. You are not allowed to live there, you are only allowed to think back in order to move forward, heal and forgive yourself. If you find yourself living there, in those shitty moments, I am going to need you to drop what you are doing and go back to step 6, you know, the one where you said you were truly ready to make a change. Yep, that one, read it back over and don't be a bitch. We are here to move forward and begin the beautiful process of self-love. So, we get to remember the moments we had, how they made us feel, where we were in our lives and make the decision to move forward.

Once you have taken the time to complete this list, read it over, several times if you have to. Relive each moment, as painful, embarrassing and hurtful as it may be, really think on each moment and picture it in your mind.

Now, the fun part. Fuck those moments, you don't live in the past and neither is your brain going to from this point forward. Those moments do not define who you are, nor do they define your future.

Remember, just because you were on the wrong way before does not mean you have to be on that way forever. You were allowed to have your bitchy moment and curse. You were allowed to make a not so great decision. You were allowed to have a rough day. That does not define who you are. It never has, you just allowed it to, and it will never again.

Moving forward, you get to practice making decisions based on love, rather than fear and hate. You get to make better decisions for yourself because you love yourself.

So, these moments you are remembering on and thinking about, are going to be gone. You will take with you only the lessons you learned from them, and the most important of those lessons is this: You made these decisions and had these moments because you were unaware of how to truly love yourself. You are responsible for them, however, you will now be responsible for the decisions you make out of love.

You get to celebrate the fact that you are moving on from your previous way of thinking, you get to celebrate your new mindset and the fact that you are moving forward; remember, love will be the basis for all things. What you are thinking of yourself and others, how you move, what you eat, how you treat yourself, who you choose to spend time with, literally everything will come from love.

How fucking badass is that?!

Apologize

Now you get to begin apologizing to yourself. Up until now, you have not been making the best decisions for you, and you get to apologize to yourself.

Personally, I took my list of past moments and placed it in the fireplace. I had a night with myself, drank tea, sat in my own thoughts and burned that baby up. I no longer need to stay attached to it. I just have to let go, and that was my symbol of letting go.

Now, I know this sounds cliché, but I do feel like once you have looked back on all these moments and relived the pain and embarrassment, you need to be at peace with you were and who you are becoming. Whatever it means to you, tear it up and toss it in the wind (well, maybe not, don't litter), burn it up, throw it away with force – I mean, throw it, make it a scene, you are done with this part of your life – or however is meaningful for you to move this out of your life, do it. And make it a celebration! Simply because it is.

Say to yourself out loud, I am forgiving myself for my past and not loving myself truly. I know now it is my responsibility to make my future fully about love and let go of fear. I apologize for not being the best me I could be to myself.

It also helps to tell someone you are in the process of forgiving yourself. Talk to them about how you are making a list, reflecting and moving on. Explain how this makes you feel, what emotions you are experiencing as you move forward, what you thought about your past, and how you plan to move on. Not only is this loving to yourself, but you may also inspire someone to make the decision to forgive themselves as well.

I took this as my direct obligation and told everyone. If someone asked me why I wasn't doing something, I would tell them I have forgiven myself for the past and I am learning how to love me and make the best decisions for myself. I know, most people thought I was crazy, but I don't care. Their opinions of my expedition are none of my business. This became something so close to my heart, that I took it in every chance I could. I realized how great it felt to really forgive myself and move on, and therefore, I wanted everyone to feel this way. I hope that you, too, will feel this way. But understand, not everyone is at this place, and you may annoy some people. Annoy them anyway.

Now, take time to truly sit with yourself and understand fully what it feels like to forgive. Just a warning: you may end up in tears at the end of this little sit with yourself. Practice having gratitude for this expedition and your new mindset about yourself. Wear something you love that makes you feel great, sit at home or take yourself to a restaurant where you can nourish yourself with beautiful food. Take yourself to get a coffee, or a pedicure and just be. Look the way that makes you feel authentic, whether it is a dress or a hat and flip flops. There is no correct way to do this, only the way that makes you feel at your absolute best. I do implore you to do this alone, though. It is difficult to reflect on yourself when you are with others.

This may sound like such a silly task, but it is incredibly important to let forgiveness to yourself sink in fully. Do not allow anyone or anything to stop you from taking this time, it is yours and a fresh start to making decisions for yourself and being true to you, loving you fully.

Close Encounters of the Doubting Kind

This is going to be the time when most people are questioning your choices and your expedition. This will be the time you will be criticized the most – or at least, I was. This will be a true test of how serious you are about changing your life for yourself.

It is insanely hard to keep going when people are questioning you, judging you, telling you they are scared for you, or just plain being pissed at you for not putting them first anymore. That is not a loss on me. I know it is hard. I know it can make you take a step back from your expedition. I know all of this, but I am here with you.

Here's the thing. This is not their expedition. It is yours. They do not have to understand what you are doing. They do not have to be happy or supportive. You are stronger than all of their opinions. Your new mindset is changing your life and that is far more powerful than other people. You are becoming a better version of yourself and those who love you will see that, those who don't are not going to be a part of it. Plain and simple! And all of this is alright, and it will get easier to deal with.

Grant Cardone says when people start questioning you or saying they are scared for you, is when you are on the right track. That is when you need to keep going, keep pushing, because you are truly on to something astonishing.

This step is going to take some time, I recommend you taking all the time you need for this. You may move beyond the past quickly and it may come easily for you, or it may take months. Take the time to ensure you are doing it for yourself and committing to forgiveness. The only way this will deeply impact your life is if it is real, open, honest and true to your authentic self. You cannot push past this step. Think about how many times you have read something and thought about it but did not put it into action. My goal is for you to take massive action toward this step. My goal for you is to see you forgiving yourself to your core.

Same Situations

Once you have gone through this entire step, you get to make better decisions for yourself. The same situations may arise that had you making decisions out of fear and hate. People may try to get the best of you. You get to use your new-found love for yourself to make a decision you will not have to look back on as the wrong one.

If someone pisses you off, you get to make decisions based on love. They may be having the worst day of their lives, their mother just passed out or they just got fired, dig deep to find some love for them.

Now I get to tell a story from my own experience of choosing love. There was a period of time my husband was unemployed. His job ended and there wasn't another on the horizon; so, home he came and sat. He wasn't getting much accomplished and the growing frustration was too much for both of us. He was pissed and depressed constantly instead of making decision to choose love, I chose frustration and anger. We fought constantly. Who the fuck wants to live like that?! Not either of us. But we both just kept assuming the other was in a shitty mood and being selfish, so we continued. I made a decision to love on him and have a conversation instead of a screaming match. He explained his depression was based on the fact that he was not providing for us, that he did not feel like a man because he wasn't bringing in an income to take care of his portion of the bills and expenses. This changed my entire outlook. He was providing, just in different ways. I appreciated all he was doing, not just his income. And financially, we were doing alright, I mean, we were not striking rich, but the bills were paid, and we were still able to enjoy some extras. Once I changed my mindset to love, he was able to open up, and we were able to understand each other better. My point here is, choose love instead of fear. And always choose love with yourself first.

The same situations that set you off in the past are still going to arise. I do promise you will see less irritation in your life, because your mindset has changed, but you will still get those moments. I implore you to choose love in these moments. Just like everything else, this is a muscle and you will have to work it, but the more you do, the more you will see how forgiveness of your past and self-love has wholly changed your life.

Some questions to think on:

- What have I done in the past that was harmful to myself?
- What have I done in the past based on fear and hurt?
- Have I ever made a decision purely for myself and out of love? How did that feel, and how can I duplicate that in my life?
- How did I feel making decisions based on fear and hurt?
- Do I think of these situations often, even if it was years ago?
- What would make me purely happy in this moment – think of everything – what would I be wearing, how would I be thinking, what types of people would I be around, what would I be doing for a living?
- How do I get to make amends to myself for my previous actions?
- What can I do moving forward, to make decisions based on love?

Featured Female – Shannon McCormack

This is ME

Whew, I honestly can say I have no remembrance of how Shannon and I met. I think through a mutual friend; or maybe playing in an adult kickball league.

Either way, she is one of the most cherished people in my life. She has the most giant heart but takes no shit, and that was something I initially envied about her. She keeps a level head and worked herself into the person she has always wanted to be, and for me, that is the ultimate form of self-love. I am so grateful for her friendship, which is so pure; I am eternally grateful she said yes to sharing a piece of herself with me and you all.

Who are you as a human?

I'm a teacher, a dog mom, and part of an amazing family both chosen and not.

What do you do for a living? Why do you choose it?

I'm a special education teacher of kids with autism specifically. Honestly, I didn't choose this. It chose me; in the form of a little guy who decided my lap was the best place for him to sit. Best interview ever!

Why do you think people lack self-love?

Simply because we were taught that doing things that promote self-love is selfish. Especially women. We were born being taught to care for others.

What are you currently working on that is bringing you joy?

My business.

When you are at peace what are you doing? What does that look like?

I'm drinking coffee, surrounded by pups, and reading a book.

What does self-love mean to you?

It means being peaceful with who I am right now. Not who I was or who I want to be. But the person I am in this moment. And loving her regardless of her flaws.

Why do you think self-love is important?

Since I've learned that without it, I cannot care for anyone else. I cannot truly be happy. I need to love myself to make the changes I want to see in the world.

Do you remember the moment you realized how to love yourself? Will you share that experience?

I do! I was in my car. And it was a really bad day. I was driving home and trying so hard not to cry. I had somewhere to go and things to do. People were waiting for me. The act not trying to cry was physically hurting me; as my throat hurts. My eyes hurt. My hands were gripping the wheel so hard they were white. Then I just said, "fuck it." I pulled over and called the people waiting for me to cancel the meeting. I told my husband I'd be late. I went to the park and I just sat in my car and cried. Just because I needed to take care of what I needed. I needed to love myself in that moment and not worry about everyone else. From that moment, I've made sure that I'm ok at all times.

What does your support system look like?

It's amazing. Family is my lifeblood, but I've also recently found the most wonderful tribe of women. I can talk to any of them about anything and I've never felt more supported in my life.

Tell me about your journey to love.

I'm not ready for this yet.

*As the author, I am pausing here for a moment to give love and light to Shannon with this question…it takes a tremendous amount of courage not only to answer, but also to recognize when you are not ready. You fucking rock, girl. Unpause.

What is your single most embarrassing moment?

Dear lord, I farted at the gynecologist in the middle of my pap smear.

How did you embrace your self-perceived flaws?

I used to hate them. But now, I see them as a way to better myself daily.

You are going to dinner…where do you go and what do you eat?

Ohjah steak house! Fish, scallops, steak and noodles.

Do you believe a higher power is at work in your life? What impact does that have?

My mom. I don't believe in God or religion, but I have to believe she's somewhere watching out for me.

What is your number one piece of advice for women learning to love themselves?

Take your time figuring it out. Don't rush. Do what work for you and then don't give up on it.

How can women connect with you?

Email: shannonmccormacklv@gmail.com

Facebook: Shannon McCormack

Chapter 9:

Step 9: Let go of everything that does not serve you

Greatest Good

In this expedition, we get to strive to be at our greatest good. This means letting go of anything, everything and anyone who does not serve that greatest good, all of this is harming you by holding you back.

It's hard, and I know I am going to hear some whining with this one – I heard it with myself. What if I hurt someone's feelings? What if my grandmother gave me that ugly ceramic vase in the corner I am currently attempting to make look like it matches my décor and taste? What if that bad habit makes me feel better about myself – isn't that what this is about? What if I need to keep that dress from fifth grade because my mom made it and loved it on me?

Cry me a river. Do you want to get better or do you want your excuses? Do you want to experience true, everlasting, pure love for yourself or do you want to continue to bitch and moan about how you can't do this or that? How you have to keep something you dislike or have outgrown because of how someone else feels about it…hell, ask them if they want it. I bet they won't. It's your choice!

And I don't mind either way, I don't judge, it's not my job. However, if you truly want this to work the way it was intended, I want to do all I can to help you with that, and sometimes that includes being a loving interruption to your bull shit. So, suck it up, buttercup. Get rid of it!

Things

Let's start here with what I consider the easy one. Things.

Things are just that – things. They may not be easy to get rid of, but it's the easiest, I think, in this step to start ridding yourself of.

So, take stock of your things. Start to determine if they serve your greatest good, if you are keeping them around for sentimental reasons or if they are useful. This is the KonMari method of decluttering – if you are not familiar, read up on this one. It really changed my way of thinking about what I keep and what I let go. If something does not bring you joy, is not useful or believed to be beautiful, out they go. And give yourself no longer than five seconds to think about it, otherwise, it will pull on you.

Here are some questions for this process:

- Does this serve my greatest good? When I look at it; am I happy or does it bring me stress and uneasiness?
- Is it useful to me?
- Did someone meaningful give this to me? If so, does it bring me happiness or is it useful to me?

Let's cover the most common argument in this process – gifts. What do I do when something was a gift, I can't just get rid of it. Here's the thing with gifts; if someone gave you something as a gift – that is not beautiful or meaningful or useful to you –

that gift has already served its purpose. It was meant as a gift for you and to bring you joy in that moment. If it no longer does, it is perfectly fine to get rid of it, sell it or gift it to someone who may appreciate it or find it useful. As a thoughtful gift from someone it served its purpose the moment it was given to you, and now it gets to bring joy to someone else who will actually appreciate it and honor it than you do now.

I had two artificial plants at one point I thought were really nice and pretty and added some color to my space. Over the course of years – YEARS people – I grew to realize they were constantly collecting dust and were impossible to clean – and they were horribly artificial, I mean, they were clearly fake and a very odd shade of green no plant should ever be. They really were not that pretty, mostly I think, artificial plants, unless really well done, are cheesier than anything.

A real plant brings life to your home and most will clean the air.

Think before you fake. Seriously, there should be rules around this. If you do decide to fake it, make sure you spend some money and get the realistic looking small ferns or succulents (those things look fake anyway) and be sure to clean them often. I digress.

Once I realized they were more of a pain in the ass for me, I still couldn't let them go. Like, what would I put in that space? It would look way too empty. Finally, one day, I told myself to throw the fucking things away! And I did. Now, I have an empty shelf and honestly, that empty shelf brings me much more joy than that damn artificial plant. It felt great. This is when I realized this whole joy around lightening your load. It made me feel so happy to not stare at those terrible things any longer.

I started on my mission, if it didn't make me happier, serve my greatest good or have purpose in some ways, it will be gone! I didn't allow myself more than 5 seconds to even think about (I'm looking at you, Mel Robbins – 5 Seconds Rule). As I kept going, I found myself feeling freer – and happier. How strange is that? Getting rid of things made me happy, it made me feel fulfilled. I finally get this minimalist lifestyle. Well, somewhat, I won't be living in a tiny home – ever, but I will have minimal things cluttering up my space.

Sentimental items were a little trickier. It was hard, but I forced myself to really think about it. Had I even seen that vase – yes that was mine – in a year. It was in a closet, collecting more dust. Off it went. I bought a small plastic tote, and anything I couldn't find in my heart to get rid of, I gave it the tote test. Did it fit in the tote? Cool, it is safe. If not, it went as well.

Take stock. Be serious. And let it go! They are just things. You don't need about 80% of them, I promise. And once you start, it will be hard to stop.

Don't forget your car and devices in this as well. Are you really going to take off to that dream job or meet up with amazing people in a vehicle that is cluttered and holding you down? No, you will not! And I promise, your phone and computer do not need everything they currently contain, downsize your apps, save the photos you love and delete the ones you don't. You cannot use that device for the greatest good if it is being weighed down by old photos and useless apps you used one time, which you probably might use another time – clue is, you probably won't. Get rid of them, and allow that device space to bring in some awesomeness.

The more you let go of, the more space will be created for amazing, beautiful things to come into your life.

People

This may be the hardest of them all.

Think of the people you complain about most often – I know you have them. It's ok. I do it, too. Those are the first ones who need to be on the list of possible eviction.

Think about the people who are constantly demanding of you, yet show nothing to return your commitment to them.

Think of the ones who show no signs of concern when you are ill, when you need someone to lean on, or are experiencing pain in your life.

Think of the ones who are constantly complaining to you about others. I'll tell you this, if they are constantly complaining to you about others, they are most likely also complaining about you to others. Keep that in mind.

Think of the people who just constantly complain or make excuses about their lives and how they could "never do that." The ones that always want something more but make every excuse not to do the work to get them. The same ones that knock you down for having the motivation to get there. The ones that are scared for you, or worried about you because you are making big changes.

Think of the people who are so content with being mediocre, they judge others for attempting any improvement. Or just the people who judge others in general.

Have you heard that quote about how you are most likely to be the 5 people you spend the most time with? Do you want to be like any of these people? If not, I suggest you start distancing yourself just a bit and venture out to find some new wonderfully supportive and positive people.

The beauty of this process is the more you talk about it, the more you improve yourself, the more these types of people tend to drift away. The more you say no to things that will not make you happy, the more these people move in another direction. The more you start making yourself your number one priority, the more these types of relationships tend to organically drift apart. And you better allow this to be a beautiful thing. They may get pissed off at you, talk shit when you are not around and make fun of your expedition, but remember.... what they do is none of your business. You get to let it roll right off your back.

They may even blame you for their shortcomings in the area of self-love or success. They may yell at you or treat you badly. They are coming from a place of hate and fear, and you are no longer there, you only deal in love now; so, you will naturally move away with peace in your heart. It can be insanely difficult at first. You may cry and it may break your heart just a bit, but I promise you the outcome is worth it. Allow yourself time to mourn the relationship and move on. They will either begin to understand, or they will not, either way – none of your business.

Also remember, you are in a place of love, and that means supporting them the best you can from a distance.

Now, think of the people who showed up for you when you were not expecting it.

Think of the people who went out of their way for you, who took time out to make something happen for you. Think of the people who made you feel special. Think of the people who support you and encourage your progress, whether it benefits them or not. Think of the people who motivate you to be your greatest good. Think of the people who are always happy for major events in your life, regardless of what that means to them, the ones who cheer you on irrespective of where they are in their own lives, because they want you to be your happiest, best self.

Those are your people. You get to start pouring into them more. You get to do the same for them and watch your mindset change and your attitude flip. Watch that negativity slip away. It is magical, and can only be experienced, not explained.

This is the hardest process. Maybe the hardest in this entire expedition. But it will be the most beneficial to you. Of anything to accomplish here, this is the one. Once you drift away from toxic humans, your toxicity falls away and your life dramatically changes. Again, this is not something that can be explained, but only experienced to know how it truly feels. So, get after it, bear down and go.

Habits

Ah, the dirty little habits. We are going to talk all habits here.

The internal ones: negative self-talk, negative talk about yourself to others, gossiping, judging others and yourself, criticizing, the list goes on and on.

The external ones: smoking, drinking, indulging in bad

relationships, involving yourself in activities that make you unhappy, people pleasing, this one goes on and on as well.

The habits you have that do not make you feel good about yourself. If you are speaking poorly of yourself, whether to yourself or to others, think about how that makes you feel, really. It may be in a joking manner, but deep down, how does it make you feel? How are you taking care of yourself if you are doubting or judging yourself? Que in: you are not. You are also giving others permission to view you in the same light you view yourself. The more you tell yourself and others the bad, the more you and others believe it. The more you push yourself away from beneficial relationships, including the one with you. What would you say if your best friend repeatedly called themselves fat or lazy? You would most likely tell them to stop it, right? Do the same thing for yourself, and surround yourself with people who will not allow such.

Think about the habits you have created. They may have been around since childhood – my nickname as a kid was chubby, try working around that one! – and it will take a little longer to remove the bad habit and replace it with a habit that makes you feel good.

For example, you tell yourself you are not good enough for....name it, the guy, the girl, the job, etc. Every time you have this thought pop up, recognize it and flip it on yourself. Give yourself a list of things you ARE good at, things you have accomplished, and people you have helped. Flip the script on the negative self-talk. Once you make this a habit, negative self-talk will diminish, and positive self-talk will start to become the new habit. The only way to kill a lie is with the truth. For every negative emotion you experience about yourself, think of two positive emotions, and constantly repeat those positive emotions to yourself, daily, hourly if you need to. You will begin to kill the lie with the truth about yourself.

I have always given myself the role of a worrier. I worry non-stop, and if there is nothing to worry about, I worry about why there is nothing to worry about. It is a sick cycle, and I told myself the same story over and over again. I am just a worrier, I will always be this way; I just have to plan and strategize so my worries become less. Until I found myself on the side of the road, pulled over because I couldn't breathe. I couldn't breathe, yall. All from tiny little things I was allowing to take over my mind has become much bigger than they were. I am the queen of turning a molehill into a gigantic mountain. And what did it stem from? Fucking worry! I realized what I was doing. And the very foundation of fixing this issue was to flip the script and stop telling myself and others that worrier was my role in life. It wasn't and isn't. Anytime I start to feel that coming out of my mouth, I flipped the script and kill that lie with the truth - I am not a worrier. I worry, but that can be changed. I am not a worrier; I am a warrior. (Que the cheesy laughs at that one). I have gotten through so much, and the small stuff? Not that important and I will figure it out. That is my answer now every time I start to feel that worry come to the surface – I will figure it out.

And a new mantra of I will be OK. No matter what, I will be OK.

Most of the time, my worry caused anxiety over things or situations that hadn't happened yet, or were months ago, or something completely out of my control. Do you know what it is called when you worry about those things? Life stranglers! I would worry so much, and neglected to enjoy this moment. I couldn't be happy about the new house we are building because I worried on how do we transfer our utilities (yup, that small and silly), or we have to figure out the new landscaping, and hang that light and get the new couch and shop for…..you get it? I couldn't enjoy right here and now, because I was so worried about what was next on the list. Again, flip it with the truth. You deserve this moment, you earned it and you have to enjoy it. Take a breath and allow yourself to be grateful. Where gratitude exists, stress and anxiety cannot. This is a habit I am still working on, and probably will for the rest of my life.

In addition to that fucked up mess, I have been working on my habit of fostering negative relationships for years. This is so common, but you will not be aware you are doing it until you make a change for yourself. You will start to see how you involve yourself in negative relationships, simply because they make you feel good, they validate your negativity and allow you to continue on that path. At the end of it all, you know these relationships do not make you feel good and are not in your greatest good. It is time to start looking for a new tribe of people who will call you on this behavior.

I fostered toxic relationships because I needed to feel needed. I wanted to always be that person everyone loved and could depend on.

So much so that I was neglecting myself and anything I wanted in life, to bend over backwards for others, who rarely returned the favor, and who did not support major goals in my life, mostly because it would not benefit them. I still bend over backwards and go out of my way for people, but for the right ones. The ones who will not only, but more likely return the favor, who are my biggest cheerleaders and who want nothing more than to see me be at my very best.

All habits have the ability to change, and for the better. Take some time to journal about what habits you recognize popping up in your life, and how you can turn them around to a new, more productive, and happier you.

Remember, you get to rewrite the script at any time to say anything you need it to say.

Try writing yourself a "to-don't" list, to go along with those "to-do" lists you have. What would you put on a definite "to-don't" list and stick to?

Here are some questions to ask yourself in this step:

- What has been weighing down my life?
- What are things do I need to eliminate from my life?
- Why do I feel this way about these things?
- Who is involved in my life that is not serving my greatest good?
- How can I take a step back from these relationships?
- What habits are not attributing to my greatest good?
- How can I change this habit to support my good?
- What will my life look like, once I eliminate what is not serving me? How will I feel?
- Do I need support in this step?

Featured Female – Abby Dunn

This is ME

I met Abby while we were both pushing hard in our mentorship group, we were paired as buddies from the start, and we connected instantly. She was leaving her safe job to take on a role that would better fit her life, which she has now turned in to exactly what she wants and needs. She is honest, and will always tell you exactly what is needed, even if it is hard to hear. We joke that I jumped in a car with a stranger, we had never met in person when she picked me up from the airport for a retreat, no questions asked! I am so honored she said yes to being a part of this book – she is one of the reasons it exists, and I am so excited to continue to watch her growth and see all her accomplishments!

Who are you as a human?

I am a wifey and a dog mom! I am super independent, but hate to be alone (yes that is a thing!) I dream of being a mom to a human kiddo and can't wait until we take that step in our lives. * I'm the wifey of a hardworking and loving husband who I love spending time with and traveling to new places! We are foodies at heart; although, I'm pretty picky but I'll try almost anything, at least once.

What do you do for a living? Why do you choose it?

I am a licensed Realtor, and currently the director of marketing for my brokerage and I am a small business consultant to a couple businesses run by local women. I didn't plan anything other than real estate, the rest have just come to me and I couldn't be more thrilled! I absolutely love linking arms with women and helping them grow their businesses!

Why do you think people lack self-love?

I think it's very hard to be reflective and love yourself when you are unhappy. It's unnatural to love yourself and life when you aren't living the dream. It takes a lot of intention to shift your mindset to be able to love yourself even

when things aren't great. I also don't believe our society really promotes and supports self-love. I think our generation is working on changing that outlook on life but it will not happen overnight.

What are you currently working on that is bringing you joy?

All of my jobs are bringing me joy. I love working with small businesses and helping them grow. We are also always doing house projects, which I love! Next up is repainting and small updates of our master bedroom.

When you are at peace what are you doing? What does that look like?

Spending focused time with Brian. I love being able to disconnect from everything else and focus on him/us and just grow our love and bond.

What does self-love mean to you?

Being happy with yourself, less negative self-talk (I think you'll always have some). Acknowledging and accepting your flaws. Following your dreams!

Why do you think self-love is important?

I think self-love is very important to improve your relationships with everyone around you, as well as yourself. I think self-love will allow you to deepen your relationship with other significantly. I also think it changes your outlook on everything around you, and you are able to see the good in life.

Do you remember the moment you realized how to love yourself? Will you share that experience?

It was very recent. I don't think it was a specific moment, but over the years from quitting my job and starting real estate, and working on my own schedule.

I realized that being less stressed at work has allowed me to really love myself and grow in my self-love and acceptance. I've connected with myself and really began focusing on being happy internally.

What does your support system look like?

I have the most supportive husband in the world! He helps me chase wild dreams and supports all my crazy ideas. My childhood best friend only lives a

few minutes away and I get to be the best aunt to her kiddo. They are a part of my family and are always there if we need anything. I've also gained 3 great girlfriends this year, that are open, honest and blunt with each other while we support our goals and grow together. Both sides of our families are also super supportive and we talk on a regular basis. I am incredibly lucky to have an amazing support system.

Tell me about your journey to love.

It has only been over the last year that I've realized how much I didn't focus on self-love. I was worried about work all the time and would bring the stress home, which bled into my relationships with everyone. I realized what I wanted out of life and worked really hard to make progress towards that dream, so I can set myself up to be happy and love myself forever.

What is your single most embarrassing moment?

I truly don't know. I always regret anytime I get an attitude with Brian in front of people.

How did you embrace your self-perceived flaws?

This year has really allowed me to work on this. I've struggled with weight and body image, but I've learned this year about dressing for my body, and embracing my love for food and eating out. My husband and I really enjoy eating out, I've come to accept that I will NEVER be as thin as I was growing up, and I'm ok with that. It's a long road of self-acceptance and having positive self-talk, and realizing my priorities in life.

You are going to dinner...where do you go and what do you eat?

TACOS! Anything Mexican is my #1 go to for every day eating out. We love Habanero's a small locally owned place. If it's a fancy date night, we go to Martini and get mozzarella cheese app (IT'S AMAZING!!!) and a steak!

Do you believe a higher power is at work in your life? What impact does that have?

I struggle with this. I think I do, as was raised in the church and plan to raise my future children in the church, but I don't have the relationship with God (or higher power) that a lot of people do.

What is your number one piece of advice for women learning to love themselves?

Your journey is going to be unique. Do not compare yourself to everyone around you. Use a support system but don't compare, especially on social media. Be open with friends, family, significant other, etc. with your progress.

How can women connect with you?

Email: abbydunn17@gmail.com

Facebook: Abby Dunn

Instagram: @_abby.dunn_

Website coming 2019!

*At the time of publication, Abby IS going to be a new mommy to a human kiddo!!! I am ecstatic for you, friend!

Featured Female – Chelsi Longworth

This is ME

I met Chelsi through a mutual friend. I loved watching her drive to help others, she organizes so many volunteer opportunities with local charities, she brings people together, and she loves on people harder than most I know. She has the biggest heart, and the most honest soul. She definitely isn't scared to tell you the truth. If she values you as a human, you will be her forever friend.

Who are you as a human?

I am a lover of tea, good deeds, my family and friends, and new adventures! My favorite thing in the world to do is laugh. It cures all!

What do you do for a living, and why did you choose it?

I am an Executive Assistant to a high profile Las Vegas influencer. I LOVE my job. I word for a non-profit that was created to enhance Las Vegas as the #1 destination for all sustainable events. We are pretty much Las Vegas Ambassadors. I didn't originally choose this career path, but I feel like my life is a series of "FALLING" into place and making the best of what happens. Ah! Doesn't really sound like a career path that I chose, but as much as a career path that chose ME!

I am and always have been a caretaker. I grew up the eldest of 4 girls, my mom was widowed at a young age, and as the eldest, I took it upon myself to be the caretaker to my siblings and my mother at times. The reason this is relevant is because of my position; I am doing the same thing I have always done. Make sure that it gets done! Take care of the small details and fix problems as they arise, without concerning the hierarchy.

Why do you think people lack self-love?

We live in a time where we are expected to be everything to everyone, and that doesn't leave much time for self-love. I don't think it's lacking, but I do think that in the scheme of things we tend to put that at the bottom of the list.

Women are told to be strong, independent, successful, doting wife, mother, great friend and honestly, that is a lot for us. We are supposed to work like we don't have kids, but act like we don't work. Where IS the time for self-love?

What are you currently working on that is bringing you joy?

I volunteer at a local hospital in the pediatric playroom once a week for 4 hours. I have a really long Tuesday. However, I LOVE being there. I don't save lives, but I help kids take their mind off what they are going through.

When you are at peace, what are you doing? What does that look like?

Sounds silly, but sometimes, I am at peace when I am cleaning or cooking. There is something extremely fulfilling in taking care of my family. On the flip side, I also like to hangout with my friends, go to a concert, travel, watch a sport game. I am at peace in lots of varying ways, but it also depends on my mood. My mood changes and that means what give me peace also changes. There isn't a rule book, just a heart's desire.

What does self-love mean to you?

Self-love to me, means being happy with who I am, and where I am. We tend to be hardest on ourselves. I am certainly one who is learning to give myself a break. I'm growing, evolving and even the hiccups have a lesson if you are

receptive to learning it. Self-love is making a mistake, and cutting yourself some slacks. We tend to give others more of a break than we give ourselves. Why is that?

Why do you think self-love is important?

Self-love is the most important love. If you can't love yourself, you are in no position to love others. Sounds simple and cliché, but that is the honest truth.

Do you remember the moment you realized how to love yourself? Will you share that experience?

I don't remember an exact moment that triggered the lightbulb, but I do remember a time in my life when I realized that self-love was lacking. I was allowing people to influence my happiness with their troubles. I was trying to help someone through a difficult time, and during this process, I was neglecting myself. I was allowing their problems to affect my sleep, home life, and even work. I did not set boundaries, but one day I snapped. I finally spoke up for myself and exactly what you would think happened. They were not interested in how I felt or what I had to say. That is when I started to realize that I am an energy sponge. I soak in things around me and I need to be careful whom I let in.

What does your support system look like?

Depending on what I am needing or what I am feeling, I have wonderful friends and family that are supportive of whatever I am going through. I don't have a support system, but many support systems. Let's be honest, a significant other isn't interested in all the things you and your friends talk about and the other way around. You need to know who to go to. If I have a sensitive issue, I am not going to go to my blunt. But rather, I am going to go to the friend that can be honest, with caring advice.

Tell me about your journey to love.

I have been in many different relationships. I loved and learned from them all.

Each one taught me what I was looking for in a lasting relationship. The journey to love continues even after you have found it. It keeps evolving, and honestly, it will continue until my last breath.

What is your single most embarrassing moment?

I have a lot of embarrassing moments, but none stick out as the most embarrassing. I get embarrassed when I am being maliciously singled out. I hate feeling like people are laughing at me.

How did you embrace your self-perceived flaws?

Most visible flaws are "fixable" or you can conceal; however, if you are battling an internal flaw, sometimes you have to switch up the routine. Help someone, volunteer somewhere. Once you realize that you are the ONLY one of your kind, you realize you are not flawed. You are unique!

You are going to dinner...where do you go and what do you eat?

My guilty pleasure is Sushi Loca. They have a tomato roll that one die for! SO GOOD!

Do you believe a higher power is at work in your life? What impact does that have?

I am not religious; however, I am spiritual. I believe that the energy you put into the universe comes back to you.

What is your number one piece of advice for women learning to love themselves?

Love yourself by keeping company with the movers, the shakers, the dreamers and the ones that believe in you, even when you don't believe in yourself. Half the battle is cutting loss of the toxicity that you are allowing to keep space in your head and by your side.

How can women connect with you?

Email: chelsilongworth@gmail.com

Facebook: Chelsi Longworth

Instagram: chelsibelle702

AMBER HAEHNEL

Chapter 10:

Step 10: Be aware and shut down old behaviors

AMBER HAEHNEL

Be aware

Step 10 is going to be the one you get to practice your whole life. You get to continue coming back here and working it.

After you have finished these steps and move forward, you will have experiences of reliving old behaviors and moments. You may even completely forget about these steps. I cannot tell you how many times I read words, and thought them over, really loved the concept, but as life went on, I totally forgot what I read and the principles behind it. We get to make sure this is not the case here.

Once you get through this, move forward and continuing living, you get to remind yourself daily of this journey and these steps. You get to write them down and put them on your mirror, so you see them every day. You get to set alerts in your phone to remind you to think. You get to journal each day, so you remember to check your behavior. You get to check in with your person or group and allow them to hold you accountable.

Daily growth is where it is. This isn't about reading the steps, applying each one and then, voila, we are perfect! Nope, and perfection is not the destination here, it never should be, it is unattainable, and will leave you feeling discouraged. The destination is learning and applying daily growth. Taking each day, remembering what our expedition is, and making a commitment to our greatest good.

In this step, you get the option of going back to step 4, reviewing each thing you wrote down and taking massive action to get better with these items each and every day.

Every time you have a fucked-up thought, a limited belief, an insecurity that creeps up, it is time to revisit this step and put all that shits in check. Check your brain, take some quiet time and remember why you started this expedition in the first place.

Reach out to your person or tribe and let them know what you are feeling, and ask for support – if asking for support is tough for you, get over yourself. We get to have an amazing system of support from others going through the same process, and we get to take time to connect with them and let them in.

This is such an important step in this expedition. To remember where we are going and continue on the path, regardless of fuck ups, because they will happen, that I can promise you.

Look, this doesn't happen overnight, and it takes a shit ton of continued work. There are going to be days when our old self, our place of hate, comes back in and tries to take over again. It is not a question of if this is going to happen, because it will. This is when we get to reflect on the time we took in steps 1 through 9, the progress we have made and the decisions we have changed, and realize how far we have come; then, make the decision of whether to stay that way or if we are going to regress and allow all this work to waist.

I promise you, if you practice this every day, and put in the effort required, it will get easier over time. The negative voice and behaviors will continue to diminish more and more over time, and the expedition will become one of love, and hate will no longer have a place.

However, this will take time, energy and effort. We have control of only two things, our attitude and our effort. And it is going to take a change in both to get where we need to be. And for the sake of your brain and heart, please let go of attempting to control anything else, you can't, and it will make you crazy – I tried, and it made me crazy. Focus on your attitude and your effort – period.

Fuck ups

We are allowed to have fuck ups along the way. It is all part of the process, and it is going to test your commitment to yourself. It is up to you whether you pass the test and continue on or allow it to swallow you up and go back to living a loveless life. Again, no one can do this for you. Even the person or tribe you chose to support you. They can be there for support and accountability, but the work is on you. Feel the pressure yet? You should. This is a big freaking deal, and without commitment, step 10 will rear its ugly head and you will falter. Now, the test is if you falter, are you going to hop back on and keep going, or have a pity party for yourself and retreat to your old life?

Don't you think you have done too much to go back there? I mean, you have already made it to step 10, why waste all this insanely awesome energy?

And maybe you throw in the towel at this point. That's ok, too. Don't drag anyone down with you, this was your decision and you get to live with the repercussions. Take some time and start over. There is nothing ever wrong with starting at the beginning, and there will be no judgement for it. Can I tell you how many times I had to go back to step 1 in this process? I probably will have to again at some points, and that is ok.

You are allowed to falter, you are even allowed to fail sometimes, but you are not allowed to stay there for long, and you are not allowed to bring anyone else down with you.

You might stop here and never look at the next two steps or the rest of them ever again. That is ok, too, this process is just not for you. No judgement, here, sister! Maybe something else will work better for you. That is ok! Just please, don't bring anyone else out with you. You get to choose for yourself, but not for anyone else. You may not recommend this for anyone else and think I totally suck, and that's cool too, none of my business. Please, don't bring anyone down with you. If you make the decision, this process is not for you; so, make it with love and move on. And of course, I will still be here cheering loudly for you to be your greatest good!

If you have made it here, and you are sticking around for the long haul, hell to the yes! Again, make sure you are making the decision out of love as well.

Honestly, there were in a few times in this process for myself, I said fuck it. I thought it was stupid to try to move on, I just kept going back to where I was. I called up that old friend to chat, mostly because I missed the drama; like, what do we really have in life if there isn't some sort of dramas?! I will tell you, we have an actual life of happiness, worth and goodness. That phone call was enough to knock me right back to where I needed to be, and reminded me why I let some people go.

I truly believe I was having withdrawals from the gossip and negative talk, it was so easy to fall right back, there was no effort there, no expectation, and no truth. It just flows out of you without much thought, which is nice sometimes, not to have thought. And I do feel like this is an addiction, and one that is incredibly difficult to kick for good. It just feels nice to bond with people, right? To have the same complaints and be able to sit and listen to one another. It is also full of hate, lies, guilt and meanness no one should live their life there permanently, literally zero growth can happen in this place. It is toxic! However, I kept finding myself back in that place, with multiple people talking about other people.

There is a quote, "Great Minds Discuss Ideas; Average Minds Discuss Events; Small Minds Discuss People." Mean people talk about people, and do you want to be the mean girl? You don't have to be a mean girl to wear pink on Wednesdays, we can do that all on our own.

I had walked away from people I felt to be toxic for my growth; however, just like any addictive behavior, it is easy to fall back into it the second you feel like you are dragging, or not growing enough, or they call and ask where you have been. There goes the guilt and I was back at square one with them listening to toxic conversations. The first thing I noticed happening, though, I fell quiet. I listened to what they were saying but stopped indulging back with them. I started to realize how terrible I felt just being a part of it all. This made it easier each time to distance, and honestly, since I stopped indulging their need, they were able to distance as well, and it made it a much easier transition.

It is a slippery slope, one time is full of happens and all of a sudden ten of those negative habits are back in your life. Once I allowed the toxic people back in, I noticed I was also holding on to things I knew I did not need, and ideas I knew were not productive. I started that sick worry/anxiety carousel again, and my thoughts were reverting to self-hate instead of self-love. It is amazing how one decision can make everything fall apart – but only if we let it. That is the beauty I kept forgetting as I kept going back to step 1 – this is all up to me, and whenever I feel the need to change the script, no matter how many times I had changed it in the past – I got to make the decision to do so, and do it with joy in my heart. Each time I started to feel like a failure and then I would feel so great to start again, I felt so new and refreshed.

I tell you this, so you know I am right here with you. Just because I designed this for myself and have gone through it for myself, I am teaching it others does not mean I am one sort of a perfect example. I still use each step every day, I still revert to where I need to be at that moment or season in my life. I still get in my own head sometimes and must take back my decisions. Again, perfection is not the goal here, it is unattainable. We are striving for progress and small improvements each day. That is all I ever hope for myself, and all I ever want for you as well.

The impulses of the past no longer have control over you. You are solely in control of yourself now. You, and only you, have the power to pull yourself back to a place of love. Allow that to be a celebration for you, something that is empowering and beautiful!

The second you see yourself going back to those old places, those old people and habits, it is time to check yourself. Take a time out – push the pause button and reflect. If you need to go back, do it. There is nothing wrong with that. Just remember why you started, stay connected to your truth, connect with your support and stay at the course, no matter what step that lands you to. No one is going to tell you a timeframe to accomplish the steps, as you get to decide how they work for you. But make the decision, don't sit for too long. You have come entirely too far here.

Remember, you are not allowed to live in your setbacks, you get to sit with them, reflect, take them in and move on. You cannot live there.

Some questions to reflect on:

- Is this hard for you? If yes, what is making hard?
- Is it worth throwing in the towel at this point?
- Would something else be working better, and who do I get to ask for suggestions?
- Who can I reach out to for support?
- Am I listening to old thoughts?
- How can I change old thoughts and behaviors to reflect where I am today?
- Do I need to go back to previous steps and start again there?
- What is my ultimate goal?
- How did I decide to commit to this program? Do I need to decide again?

Featured Female – Kendall Boehm

This is ME

The first time I met Kendall, was through a mutual friend, and she was insanely pregnant with twin boys. At some points over the next couple of years, we travelled together from our businesses – to New Orleans and Indiana – and grew incredibly close. She had two more tiny humans and I love them all so dearly. She has been a savior to me and one of the best humans I have the privilege of knowing on the planet. She is the reason I firmly believe people are put in our lives for a purpose. She did not only allow me fully into her life, but the life of her entire family as well.

Who are you as a human?

I love to hear about you, your life and your experiences. I love to connect with similar experiences and learn about life that I have no clue about. I love to be the life of the party. I wear my heart on my sleeve most of the time, but learn fairly quickly about being taken advantage of. Prior to having kids, I was a professional at walking away, i.e, you screw me and you'll never hear from me again, having kids blurs that line.

What do you do for a living? Why do you choose it?

I am a snack bitch.... I mean, a stay at home mom! I chose to stay home for financial reasons. Having twins in daycare is a huge expense, and then add two more. I'd be working to lose money.

Why do you think people lack self-love?

Insecurities from previous life experience. Consciously known or not.

What are you currently working on that is bringing you joy?

Taking time for myself. I could literally open my eyes and have to serve someone or something else all the way until I close my eyes again. I intentionally schedule working out, make time for convos with friends and do my best to make time for a time out of the house.

When you are at peace, what are you doing? What does that look like?

I am surrounded by friends and family. Simply being with them makes me at peace. The convos, laughs, tears, and connections.

What does self-love mean to you?

Being more than OK with who you are inside and out, AND making time to improve upon those things.

Why do you think self-love is important?

You cannot pour from an empty cup. You will never make anyone or anything happy until you are yourself.

Do you remember the moment you realized how to love yourself? Will you share that experience?

Deep question! ☺☺ No clue of the moment when I realized it. Somewhere in the blur of becoming a new mother AGAIN.

What does your support system look like?

Amazing mom, dad, brother, moms side extended relatives, step parents AND ride or die friendships (even when they are mainly via social media/test) each and every one of them plays a huge role in my support system.

Tell me about your journey to love.

Gah. Again, so deep. I grew up knowing self-love. I don't know how or why, but that's the way it was. I carried that into the adolescence and 20s. It wasn't until I married and took on the "baggage" of someone else that I started to doubt that. Only to be personified by becoming a new mom over and over again in a short period of time. After my 3rd baby in 15 ½ months and the reality that my husband was all sorts of fucked up with his own issues of a previous divorce, parenting (or lack thereof) and just life in general, it hit me like a ton of bricks that I would never be able to love him without truly loving myself and my own journey.

What is your single most embarrassing moment?

Can I say I've lost count? Admitting over and over that I've "allowed" my husband to continue to be a compulsive gambler, a dad that every single night he screams at our four kids that they're horrible, out of control, and brats...all while giving them candy to try and reward or change their behavior.

How did you embrace your self-perceived flaws?

Social media mom groups! Reading those other moms with multiple little kids were experiencing the same things.

You are going to dinner....where do you go and what do you eat?

Somewhere with food haha! I literally eat EVERYTHING. Preferable if they serve alcohol. My friends and family would choose Olive Garden, Cheesecake Factory or any old bar for me.

Do you believe a higher power is at work in your life? What impact does that have?

Absolutely. I'd consider myself a believer that isn't necessarily into reading and interpreting bible verses, but has a sense of feeling that there is a higher power. A comfort in hard times, someone to "talk to" in sorrow and celebration and a grounding throughout life knowing that everything happens for a reason.

What is your number one piece of advice for women learning to love themselves?

Embrace the chaos. You are not alone.

How can women connect with you?

Email – ohannagyrl@yahoo.com

Facebook: facebook.com/boehmmom

Featured Female – Sara Irizarry

This is ME

I met Sara while hanging out at a friend's house in the summer, that mutual friend of ours is now her husband! I loved her laid-back attitude, and we connected while discussing yoga and women's role in the world. I loved that at a Las Vegas pool party we were able to have a deeper conversation about something meaningful. We have stayed connected through the years and I knew she was exactly the person I wanted to feature here. She has a career she is passionate about, a pretty cool husband and an even a cooler dog. I am grateful to have gotten to know her more over the years and honored she said yes to being interviewed here.

Who are you as a human?

I am a strong, caring woman who wants to make a positive impact on those around me.

What do you do for a living? Why do you choose it?

Health care strategy (moving America from fee-for-service to value based care). I believe we should all have access to high quality, and affordable health care. There is a lot of work to be done in this industry to improve the lives of Americans, and I love seeing the impact of people committed to that improvement.

Why do you think people lack self-love?

We are constantly surrounded by messages of how to improve ourselves.

Marketing, especially to women who have focused on physical beauty and the "ideal" we should all be trying to achieve. Our culture also rewards being busy, to a fault. In my opinion, it's difficult to find reinforcement that self-love is important and something you need to focus on. It's easier to be critical of yourself and compare yourself to those around you, because that's what we've been taught to do.

What are you currently working on that is bringing you joy?

After opening 9 clinics for seniors/Medicare patients this year, I'm working on building patient experience in the clinics. I love connecting with people and working to improve the care they are getting. I get to tap into the passion of the clinicians and teams that work in the clinics to bring their ideas to life.

When you are at peace what are you doing? What does that look like?

I have anxiety, so being at peace is tough for me. I feel the best when my life is in balance: I'm taking care of myself (eating well/exercising), I'm on the same page as my husband and communicating well with him, and I'm caught up at work driving my daily focus. When one of those pieces falls out of balance, my anxiety rears its head. I did find that I was the most at peace EVER in Bali. It was a beautiful island and everyone I spoke with was open and positive. All of the pieces of my life felt like they were easily in balance, I had great food, tons of hiking and diving, plenty of time with my husband and quiet time to work on projects I cared about, and perfect sunsets with an ocean breeze////I tried to cancel our flights back and stay for good ☺☺ but that would have knocked the work part of my life out of balance quickly.

What does self-love mean to you?

Accepting where you are today, making the time and effort to focus on growth and ensuring your emotional and physical needs are met (and that they are a priority in your life).

Why do you think self-love is important?

Your relationship with yourself is the one relationship you know you'll have your whole life. Understanding your core values, what drives you and who you want to be will direct the rest of your life and relationships. I've struggled with depression and anxiety; so, for me, a big part of self-love is mental health, and reaching out for help when needed. Self-love is being in touch with what you need and prioritizing yourself to get it. To me, recognizing that and practicing self-love will make the rest of your life easier and more fulfilling.

Do you remember the moment you realized how to love yourself? Will you share that experience?

In my early 20's I was a serial monogamist and defined myself too heavily on the success of my relationships. I moved to Ukraine when I was 28 and spent close to 3 years living on my own, in a Russian speaking village (there were maybe 3-4 people who could speak English with me), working on antihuman trafficking legislation and HIV/AIDS education. At times, it was isolating, but overall, I got the chance to truly be myself, spend plenty of time reflecting (in the - 40-degree winter weather alone) and build relationships from scratch. Communicating in a new language made me focus on what was important to me and help prioritize what I needed to learn to express myself and connect with people around me. It was a transformative time for me, and I left with the confidence to be me in any situation.

What does your support system look like?

I have a strong support system. I can talk to my husband about anything and everything and our dog, Nesta is always a comfort to me (a motivator to stay active, because he has endless energy). My immediate family all live close to me and give great career and life advice. I can count on them to be there and to give me tough love when needed. I love the fact that both of my sisters married men with local families as well, so we have a broad network of support and huge family events that bring 4 families together. I also have great in-laws (we moved in with them for 6 months while building our house and it gave us a chance to grow a lot closer). Some of my closest friendships are with other Americans I met in Ukraine. I was a three-hour drive away from the closest American, but we skyped, emailed and texted to vent and help each other through similar issues. They are some of my favorite people to visit now. They have seen me at my most vulnerable and help me become stronger.

Tell me about your journey to love.

This is a big, complex question! I see it as an ongoing journey that changes as you grow and experience different things in life. I've had big derailing moments, for example, I cheated on a boyfriend, mostly because I didn't have the strength to openly talk about our future and what I wanted. I've also had big moments that bring me closer to love. My relationship with my husband has been a huge help because he is accepting the person I am and we can talk about where we want to go together. Outside of romantic love, I have found that I am happier and more fulfilled when I support those around me and work intentionally to act and speak from a place of love. The times relationships breakdown or I've been in a fight, I can look back and see that my actions weren't coming from a place of love and as a result, my life started moving in a negative direction. To me, focusing on love is a choice you continue to make every day.

What is your single most embarrassing moment?

There are so many to choose from 😊😊 Reflecting on this question, I have embarrassing moments all over the board (I ripped my swimsuit going down a waterslide and no one told me for hours. I ended up locking myself in a bathroom and vomiting on a first date, refusing to come out. While living in Ukraine, I was informed by a friend that I had gotten a reputation as a woman with loose morals for smiling too much at men in the village) ...but, I tend to laugh at all of it.

How did you embrace your self-perceived flaws?

This is a tough one, and something I continue to work on. I like to focus on me as a whole. There's always a room for improvement, but overall I'm happy with the decisions I've made and who I am. Life isn't as simple as just removing my flaws, picking and choosing the parts of myself I want to present to the world. That would make me a different person.

You are going to dinner…where do you go and what do you eat?

Somewhere new/trendy and definitely fancy. If I'm going out, I want an indulgent meal, with a good company and a great wine to go with it.

Do you believe a higher power is at work in your life? What impact does that have?

No, I believe I'm going to get out of life what I put into it. For me, that means taking responsibility for my choices and how I impact those around me. It also encourages me to act when I see an issue, because I don't trust that "things are going to work out" without people making it happen.

What is your number one piece of advice for women learning to love themselves?

Don't compare yourself to others, embrace who you are at your core and focus on what you want from life. Also, the advice that I continue to need…be patient with yourself. I feel like I read this advice everywhere and I still need it every time I hear it!

How can women connect with you?

Facebook: Sara Irizarry

Instagram: @sarechka

Chapter 11:

Step 11: Take back your power, drop the victim mentality, and forgive others.

Taking back your power

Taking massive action on these steps is integral to this process. You must take action, massive action at that, to get where you need to be, and the time is now!

You get to take back the power to your life. You get to stop pointing fingers and blaming anyone else for what has happened thus far in your life. You get to take responsibility for everything you have encountered, including this expedition.

No one is responsible for anything in your life except for you. I suppose being born was someone else's decision and responsibility. However, you get to take responsibility for everything else. Even if you had a bad childhood, you get to take responsibility on how you have responded or reacted. If you have a shitty job, or lost your job, you get to take responsibility for however it works best for you getting a new one. If you don't have money, cannot find love, want to grow a business but don't know how, or are still finding it hard to love yourself. You get to take responsibility for all of that and more.

This is your expedition. Yes, you get support along the way and you get to take the wheel as you see fit, but it is yours. You get to live it however you want and however, it works best for you. No one else can do this for you. You are the operator of the ship, the owner of the thoughts and the worker of the heart. All of this is yours – let that be empowering to you, no scary or daunting.

You get to take this expedition and make it the best for you, but that begins with taking back your power and that is exactly what you are going to do in this step.

How? Well, you have already gone through so many of the steps and are pushing through the good, bad and ugly, and you are here, that is a huge accomplishment.

You get to take each step and throw them together to create your path to power. You have done so much already to take it back, now it is simply making the decision to keep it that way. To own it all! Make the decision, go ahead. Your life is changing.

I want to take some time to discuss the difference between reacting and responding here. In my years of therapy and counselling, I have learned to differentiate these two behaviors. I want you to learn to respond to your life – taking ownership and a calm review of what is happening, as opposed to reacting – irrational, erratic behavior in regard to what is happening. When you respond you are allowing time for your brain and heart to absorb what you are going through and come up with a decision on how to handle it. When you are reacting to something it is a knee jerk reaction rooted in emotion and not allowing your brain and heart to absorb anything. Take time when deciding how to handle your decisions. This will allow you to take back so much more of your power.

I was always the person to react, and usually irrationally to most things in life, I never allowed my brain and heart to take a moment to think over anything, I just did what I felt in the moment and it was all very emotional – usually leaning towards negative emotions, which was not the productive way of life. I got to learn over time how to take a moment and sometimes communicate to others that I needed to take a moment and collect my thoughts, so I could better respond to something. This takes time to learn, but your relationships, including with yourself, will thrive when you do.

Drop the victim mentality

This is all tied together if you cannot tell. You are no longer a victim. Victims allow circumstances to be developed for them, not to determine them for themselves. Victims allow the world to happen instead of happening to the world. Victims live in a place of fear, anger and hurt.

Not you, as you now live in a place of love. You get to drop this mentality. And if you have been working the steps up until this point, you are well on your way.

You no longer get to throw yourself a party of pity. You no longer get to act like someone or something else holds the keys to your happiness, if you haven't caught on yet, only you hold these keys. You no longer allow anything else to hold control in your life.

You are not a victim; you are the owner of your expedition. And anytime you feel like you are a victim, you get to revisit this step – and maybe step 10 as well – and remember you are well on your way, and no one owns this like you do, you are in control and you are powerful. You are a force and you make the decisions that you will no longer decide to be a victim.

This started in a difficult place for me. I have not brought this up here, yet, but my perfect example is my husband's addiction. I blamed every single thing on my husband's addiction for a long time. If I was stuck in traffic, well of course, that was his fault. If I was having a bad day, it was because he drank that day. If I was tired, it was because I had to stay up worried about him and his decisions. I was the victim in the relationship. Everything was his fault. This created an incredibly toxic atmosphere. He always felt like he could never live up to what I wanted, and I felt like he was constantly the reason for blame in everything bad that happened.

One thing I realized in this was while watching a Tony Robbins documentary, if I am to blame him for all of the bad, I had to blame him for all of the good as well. I couldn't do that; although, he wasn't contributing anything good in my mind – which of course was completely false. I blamed him if the laundry wasn't done, if I was grumpy, if I needed to pick something up but did not have time. Poor guy.

Doing this does not allow me to take responsibility for my own life, and it made our relationship a place neither of us felt safe in. I could only control my attitude and my effort, right. So, I started focusing there, and the victim mentality slowly but surely started to disappear in this respect. I started realizing where I was, and where he was and we met each other where we were. Patience and time made the change, but it was the effort I put into changing my attitude and mindset. I am not the victim. He is not to blame. I get to take ownership of my life and adjust myself. I realized he could not make me happy, or sad, or mad or any other emotion you might blame on someone else. I was the only one that could, and until I dropped the victim mentality and took my life back, nothing was going to change.

Repeat: I am not a fucking victim. I am the owner of my life and I get to call the shots. Allowing this to be placed in anyone else's hands is unfair and unrealistic. I am not a victim; I am the powerful force.

Take ownership of your life

Just another fancy way of describing what you are doing. You are taking ownership of what is yours and has always been yours. You are waking up to the fact that life is now and you get to live it. You allowed ownership of your own life to diminish; so, you have to take it back for good. You have to stand at the top of your very own mountain and know you are living this life for yourself.

Again, you are well on your way by working these steps to taking the ownership of your life and become authentically loved by yourself. Once you have taken the ownership and are making decision based on what is in your greatest good, you will feel just on how powerful this is. Another piece of this that cannot be explained, only experienced.

Make decisions based on how you feel, if you are not feeling joyful, it may be the wrong decision. Stop worrying about what other people may think of your decisions, it is none of your business what they think anyway. Determine what is making you happy based on your progress so far and keep doing more of that.

When thinking of a big life change, what do you think of first? If it is what your spouse or your parents might think, you get to reevaluate. The first thing you get to think of is whether or not it is going to move you forward and bring happiness to your life, leave out the rest and focus on yourself.

What has always been hiding in your soul? And what is keeping you from pursuing it? Make sure you take time to really think about these and move forward, based on what you want and no one else.

It may be difficult, but we have to include our spouse or partner in this as well, we cannot worry about their thoughts on what we are doing with our lives. Now, if your dream is to move to Africa and live with a tribe off the map for six years and write a book about gorillas, and that is what you are going to pursue with your whole heart, you may want to talk to your partner about this and get their input. However, if it is truly something that moves you to your core, go after it, even if everyone, including your partner, thinks you are crazy. The mark of something good about to happen is when other people think you are out of your damn mind. If that is the case, keep going.

The key to making sure you are doing something great is to embarrass yourself. We are getting into going after our dreams here, which is fantastic because that is part of this whole thing. And if it makes you embarrassed, do it until you no longer feel embarrassed to do it, or talk about it or act on it. If you are feeling embarrassment, it is because you are new at something and you have changed the course, that is the true mark you are on your way. Maybe you are embarrassed to tell people you are part of this expedition, cool. Eventually, you will lose the embarrassment of the whole thing, but in the meantime, you are showing yourself that you can push past what other people expect of you. You are pushing past the normalcy, and going outside of the box. This is growth, this is change, this is amazing!

I challenge you to embarrass yourself once per day until you no longer feel embarrassed about what you are accomplishing. Then think of something new and start all over again! Grow, my friend!

Forgive Others

This may be a difficult part of the process. But you cannot live life being weighed down by anger and resentment. And you cannot be true to yourself and loving with this hanging on your shoulders.

When you forgive others, you are not allowing or condoning the behavior, you are simply giving yourself permission to let go and let yourself move on.

I struggled with this for so long. I really thought if I forgive someone, I will be condoning their behavior and telling them what they did was alright. I thought if I forgave bad behavior or feelings of hurt, it gave permission for the person to do it all over again. Now, if you continue to forgive the same behavior over and over, allowing that person in your life, yes, you may be telling them the behavior is allowed, keep up your boundaries. However, forgiveness will never be bad for you, it will always help you heal and move forward. Forgive, hold your boundaries and move forward with love.

Forgiveness is a form of self-love, it is a form of letting yourself go, or freeing yourself from resentment, while resentment is the killer of most goodness. You simply cannot be at your greatest good when harboring feelings of resentment. They cannot live together in the same house. Get rid of it. Forgive, as that needs to happen, and whatever that means for you.

Holding on to anger is like drinking poison and expecting the other person to die. ~Buddha

Now, how do you feel about holding on to anger and resentment? Do you want to have poison flowing through you, or do you want to feel the freedom of forgiveness?

This is a mandatory step, hard as it may be. But the more you hold on to the past in any way, the harder it will be to find true happiness and love within yourself. It is time for you to feel freedom and learn to move on from the wrongdoings of others. You are not going to change what happened, but you absolutely can change your response to what has happened. Keep in mind the difference between response and react.

Start by making a list of people and things that you have been holding resentment and anger toward. And dig deep here, some of them may span back to childhood. You may still have contact with the person and you may not. What I suggest here is writing all of this down and then writing a short letter for each instance. This is for you, not anyone else; so, this does not require an act of telling someone you forgive them, that is where a misunderstanding may come in. You do not have to actually tell the person you have forgiven them, this is for you only, you can simply write it down and feel it in your heart to move forward. If this makes it easier for you, by all means, set up a time and have a talk with that person. However, the simple act of writing it down and releasing it can incredibly be powerful.

Make your list. Reflect on each. Talk to the person if needed. And let it go. One at a time, really reflects and let go. Say out loud, even just to yourself, that you have forgiven this person from the bottom of your heart, and you are ready to move on. Maybe sit in an inspirational or beautiful place while you perform this act. Make it meaningful to you and put your whole heart to it. Truly feel the freedom of forgiveness wash over you. This may take a few moments; it may take a few months. Irrespective of how long it takes, it is right for you, do not push it or force it, and make sure you are feeling it deep within.

Take a few days, or weeks if you need to after this act, in order to make sure you are truly feeling forgiveness in your heart. You do not have a deadline for this activity, it will take as long as it takes you. And if you feel the need to do it again and again in the future, do it! Again, this is for you, no one else, and will only work according to your needs and requirements.

Set up boundaries for the future, especially if you are allowing the same person you are forgiving into your space. Think of the boundaries you need to set up to keep them as part of your life, and what your rules will be for yourself in being near them. You do not need to tell them the rules or boundaries, but uphold them as you need to in order to live at your greatest good.

Policies

Think of policies you have to include in your life to lift you up to your greatest good. These can be in the form of boundaries, what you will and will not tolerate from others in your circle. What you will allow into your space, as far as things and habits. What you will expect of yourself.

One of my policies I hold for myself is saying no to what will not serve me and bring me joy. If I am feeling overwhelmed, I will reevaluate my schedule and start crossing things off that are not serving my greatest good. And in this, I decided not to have guilt in saying no, because I will not feel good about it if I say yes. And others who support me and my vision for myself, will want the same thing.

Another policy I have is not allowing my cell phone in the bedroom. This one may seem small and somewhat insignificant; however, it is serving me best at this season in my life. Doing this allows me to unwind and relax my mind without the temptation of working or cruising social media checking out other people's lives. It is my bedroom; I need to be focused on my own life. Common resistance I get from others is that they use theirs as an alarm clock, well, they actually sell those separate from a phone and some are super awesome and simulate sunlight. Also, emergencies may occur. Yes, they may, but I am not going to be able to do anything in the middle of the night but worry about anything that may come across that phone, I will be more equipped to handle it first thing in the morning.

Setting family and me time is one of my policies as well. I set the time I will spend with my family and with myself each week and no matter what else comes up for me in those times, the answer will be no, unless it is an emergency. This has done wonders for my relationship with my family as well as with myself.

Take some time to set up some policies and boundaries for yourself. What do they look like, and who will you share them with to keep you accountable? Imagine how good you will feel when you stick to things that bring you joy and allow yourself the boundaries to take care of yourself.

How are you feeling?

Journal about this step and how you are feeling. Are you ready to take back your life? Are you letting go of being a victim and allowing you to be the top priority and owing that?

Are you feeling forgiveness? What does that feel like to you?

Take some time with this step, it is so important and will likely take some time to complete. Come back when you are ready. We will be here.

Featured Female – Nellie Corriveau

This is ME

I first met Nellie doing health and fitness Coaching. She immediately grabbed my attention as Founder of NC4K, non-profit helping pediatric cancer families – that she founded at 16 years old. We connected to discuss, and her positive attitude, drive and blunt honesty made me love her instantly. When she announced her yearlong mentorship group, I jumped on board and never looked back, it is one of the reasons I am writing this book. She is a mom, an advocate, a passionate friend and mentor, Coach and sister. I will continue to be amazed by her.

Who are you as a human?

Kind and Loving.

What do you do for a living? Why do you choose it?

I support other women by brainstorming what they want out of life and then making a plan to get there…and beyond!

Why do you think people lack self-love?

The world has told them it is being selfish.

What are you currently working on that is bringing you joy?

My mentorship group and being a mommy!

When you are at peace, what are you doing? What does that look like?

I am at peace when my schedule isn't so full and I can be present with people.

What does self-love mean to you?

It means taking care of yourself, so that you can take care of others and not half ass either of them.

Why do you think self-love is important?

If we loved ourselves and even more, then that love would spill over into the world and create a crazy and amazing ripple effect!

Do you remember the moment you realized how to love yourself? Will you share that experience?

Honestly after giving birth was a true test of self-love with all the body and hormone changes. I got to learn how to be beautiful and work in progress again.

What does your support system look like?

My husband, his family, my best friends, the amazing mentorship group and soon to be coach and therapist.

Tell me about your journey to love.

I think the journey to love is ongoing and never ending, which can feel overwhelming and also exciting at times. I went from working 80 hours a week and being overweight to cutting back my hours, losing a ton of weight and investing ME with personal growth courses and conferences. Then we got pregnant! I feel so thankful for that order too because I feel like I have so many tools as a new mom that I am not sure what would have happened if I was still working 80 hours a week without taking care of my body…and add a baby into that. EK! This is the true testament of why self-love is so important too!

What is your single most embarrassing moment?

When I peed my pants in second grade, I will never forget that! LOL!

How did you embrace your self-perceived flaws?

I don't hide them anymore; they are a part of me!

You are going to dinner…where do you go and what do you eat?

Honestly, I am such a fan of grab your favorite dinner and have a fancy picnic at home with a movie.

Do you believe a higher power is at work in your life? What impact does that have?

1000% I consider myself very spiritual. I believe our energy is the most powerful super power we have. The universe loves positive and kind energy too: ☺☺

What is your number one piece of advice for women learning to love themselves?

Just fucking do it and not feel shame! Buy the outfit, go out with friends, read that book, get a massage or nails done, take a walk, drink water and eat good foods, TAKE CARE OF YOU FOR YOU. No more guilt or shame only loving action. Do you think men feel shame or guilt when they do stuff for themselves? …nope! So, why do women? It is time to shut down that conversation and step into your power.

How can women connect with you?

www.positivelyyoucoaching.com

Featured Female – Danielle Hogle

This is ME

Danielle and I first met in what seems like thousands of years ago when we were just girls on a dance team in Dayton, Ohio. We were reconnected years later via social media, where I totally thought she was super annoying – no joke. And we started doing fitness together and our friendship grew from there! She is passionate and LOVES women supporting women and empowering other women to be the best version of themselves. Honestly, she had no intention of me writing a book, but her belief in me helped me become who I am today. I am so happy she said yes to adding her voice here.

Who are you as a human?

I'm a real, raw and honest woman with a heart and passion for making a difference in the world. I am a fur mom to 2 CRAZY German Shepherds, a Britney Spears fanatic, lover of reality tv, dancing machine, that loves French fires and travelling the world.

What do you do for a living? Why do you choose it?

I am a fitness professional. I Coach women virtually; I am a certified personal trainer, and teach group fitness classes. I LOVE IT!

When I found myself 50 pounds overweight after graduating with my Master's degree, I decided I had to do something different. I didn't enjoy typical workouts. The gym wasn't for me. Eating salads weren't for me. Lifting weights weren't for me.

When I found programs and plans that worked for me, I decided to help other women just like me.

Surprisingly, I don't do this because it excites me to see people lose weight. I do this work because of the confidence I see build in women as they take time for themselves and focus on their health and fitness. They walk with more pride, they believe in themselves more, they go after big goals and dreams that they gave up in the past.

I do this work because it gives women the power and confidence they want and need to live their best lives! I genuinely believe that happiness begins with health.

Why do you think people lack self-love?

Truthfully, I think it's because society tells us to. I believe we live in a world where we are constantly told that we aren't good enough.

The magazines, movies, social media e.t.c We are faced with PERFECTION day in and day out. Companies use this. Make-up advertising tells us our wrinkles, cellulite and stretch marks need to be fixed. The doctors' offices advertise that we just need a tummy tuck. The world constantly tells us we should have and want more things and bigger houses and fancier cars and if we aren't there yet, something is wrong with us.

We find ourselves doing things, pursuing jobs and dressing certain ways, to fit in with what society wants us to do, instead of being and doing what WE really want, and it's hard to love yourself when you aren't true to yourself. And to top it all off, if we DO love ourselves the way we all want to, we are viewed as narcissistic. We're supposed to love ourselves but not be conceited making it even more challenging to really be proud of self-love.

What are you currently working on that is bringing you joy?

I'm currently working on content for a blog & YouTube channel to motivate and inspire women to appreciate their bodies as they are, take control of their finances, and love their reality.

When you are at peace, what are you doing? What does that look like?

Dancing. It's how I've always just felt at peace. It's a way to express myself.

Most days, it's me just blaring music and freestyling. Other days, it's taking time to create choreography. Other days, it's teaching a live hip hop class. It's my way of releasing everything that I feel and just being 100% authentically me.

What does self-love mean to you?

It's hard to put into words…

It means gratitude, respect, and appreciation. It means looking in the mirror with gratitude for who I am and what I'm doing.

It means respecting myself to a point where I make decisions that are right for me, which will make me genuinely happy. Respecting my heart, mind and body enough to take care of them daily. It means appreciating all of me...my "flaws," my strengths, and my body. It means being my very own best friend.

Why do you think self-love is important?

In order to be the best version of ourselves, we must respect and love ourselves. Everything starts and ends with our relationship with ourselves. If we aren't fully in love with ourselves, we can't fully love others. When we truly love who we are, we can accomplish incredible things, we wouldn't be able to otherwise and the world needs more of that.

Do you remember the moment you realized how to love yourself? Will you share that experience?

No...I think it was a journey and continues to be one. I'm not sure I believe that there's a finish line to self-love. I think it's a daily action. It's waking up every morning making the decision to practice self-love, appreciation, and compassion.

For me, it started with reading personal development books. Constantly putting positive words and thoughts into my brain to replace the negative ones.

I added in workouts and healthy foods and over time I realized that those simple things were a form of self-love. When I transformed my body through fitness, and transformed my mind through personal development; I realized I was loving myself more and more each and every day. And moving forward every day, I continue to take action towards self-love.

I truly believe that if it's not a daily practice, a habit, to focus on self-love, it will start to disappear because of outside forces. Although, that's sad, but it's also exciting because it means that we can be in control of it!

What does your support system look like?

I have a significant other of 9 years that is my best friend and biggest supporter. I have amazing parents that have always been my support system.

And I've surrounded myself with positive, successful, go-getter women that do not only support me, but also push me to be the best version of myself.

What is your single most embarrassing moment?

OMG! why am I taking forever to think of this?! Perhaps I just blocked out every embarrassing situation in my life… lol hmmmm

You are going to dinner…where do you go and what do you eat?

Whole Foods – Nashville Hot Chicken, Mac and Cheese, and Mashed Potatoes with a chocolate parfait for dessert and a lemonade.

Do you believe a higher power is at work in your life? What impact does that have?

I believe in a higher power....

What is your number one piece of advice for women learning to love themselves?

Self-love is not a final destination, it's a journey; so, wake up and take one step at a time, and be proud of the progress you make each day through your actions. Focus on YOUR self-love journey, and don't compare your story to someone else's. Decide what true self-love means to YOU and work towards that every day!

How can women connect with you?

Email: danielle@coachdaniellenicole.com

Facebook: facebook.com/daniellehogle87

Instagram: @daniellenicolehogle

Website: coachdaniellenicole.com

Chapter 12:

Step 12: Stay connected to your true self and help others

AMBER HAEHNEL

There is always something to learn from your life experiences. Look at your limitations and insecurities as opportunities for growth and helping others. Imagine life as a river, and these are the stepping stones to get across. If you can get past the eye-roll worthy comparison there.

It is time to start looking at lifeless selfishly than you have been. Contrary to popular belief, taking care of yourself is, in fact, one of the most selfless acts you have to do.

When you are in tune with your true self, you are a better human all around, and therefore, a better friend, lover, mentor, mother, father, neighbor, and everything. You are better to serve other people when you are at your greatest good and the best version of you.

You stop lying to yourself and others, you are quick to forgive yourself and others, you are easier to be around, and you start to attract other people who are in your realm of beliefs. It is an all-round happier existence.

There are absolutely no limits to what you can do with your life, and how you can be the happiest, most productive, true version of yourself. Anything you want, you get to achieve, and are fully capable of doing so. It all requires the mindset of happiness, of love over fear and of taking massive action to make it happen.

At the end of this, it gets to be you, and you alone, who wants change. You get to make the decision and truly take action on getting where you need to be and becoming the person you truly always have been.

Hell with the naysayers, and those who will criticize you; a matter of fact, you do not need those people in your life, as you are on your way to attracting a new set of people who are going to support, love and encourage you to go after everything you want. You are attracting people now who are going to fully support you putting yourself first. Wondering if someone is mad at you is a thing of the past, you are opening yourself to relationships of communication. Having people in your life who criticize and make you feel unimportant are gone, you have eliminated those who are not supportive and you are on your way to finding the tribe who lifts you up, no matter what that means to them.

Gone are those things and emotions weighing you down and making you feel heavy. You are free, light and ready to move on to a new way of living.

You are fucking unstoppable. You have everything in you right this moment to take on the world and live to your truest potential; once you have made the decision to tap into that and own it for yourself.

Staying connected

You have learned how to develop a new way of thinking, and therefore, a new type of life. Now, it is up to you to stay connected to your true self.

This is going to take time and relentless effort. Each step, including this one, must be taken seriously and acted upon with conviction, intention and purpose. Reflect on each as needed to ensure you do not slip back into old habits and thinking. Staying connected with your true self and really loving who you are is going to be needed.

Take this time to reflect on each of the steps and commit to a game plan on how you are going to stay on track.

Are you going to meditate daily and write gratitude?

How about making sure you are taking an hour per day to do something good for yourself? Even if that means sitting in silence and decompressing from the day. Or finding pockets of time to commit to your new habits, even five minutes at a time.

Are you going to keep that list from step 4 and remind yourself each day how far you have come?

Could you write down affirmations and keep them on your mirror or your desktop each day, so you are reminded of your true self?

Can you journal each day for ten minutes?

Can you practice gratitude daily in ordinary things?

Take this time to think out a plan of action. How are you going to stay committed, continue eliminating any negative from your life and stay on the path of self-love?

Helping others

This part is most exciting for me. Helping others realize their true selves and recognize self-love within themselves. No matter how far you are in this expedition of yours, you are always qualified to help someone else start theirs. You have gifts to give the world, and enough in your heart to help an indefinite number of people.

It is essential to help others get started, as it brings you back to where you started and passes on the good faith. Anyone at any time can show someone how to live their greatest good and start loving themselves more. And the beautiful part of this expedition is that you are going to start getting questions from people. Others are going to see the changes you have made and want to know more. People inherently want to be authentic and true to themselves, and as you progress, whether you talk about this expedition or not, people are going to see changes in you and want to know how they can start living their most authentic lives. They will want to know how to learn to love themselves better, all because you have been an example to them. Isn't that a gorgeous thought?

The more you talk about it, the more you will continue your expedition as well. The more you will stay true to yourself and be comfortable telling people how this has been the best expedition of your life and you will be happy to share the details. It will all come naturally. Remember that part about embarrassment? The more you discuss this, the less embarrassed you will be to tell others about it!

And we all need to share a little more about what makes us, us. We get to start sharing what makes us happiest, and how we are living up to our authenticity. We get to share how to love ourselves more. There is enough bad and negativity in the world, we get to spread the love. Imagine the world with happy, fulfilled people full of love instead of fear. Pretty gorgeous, right?

Questions to reflect on:

- How can you be of more service to people?
- What is your most valuable truth?
- What is the most important part of this expedition to you?
- How can you share that with someone in your shoes?
- How have you noticed the changes happening in you?
- Are you more helpful, and more willing to share?

We are not fucking around here, people. We have a life to live!!!

Featured Female – Dr. Sarah Schonian

This is ME

Who are you as a human?

Who I am as a human? Wow. I have asked this question to others, both personally and professionally, but until now I never quite understood how challenging it is to provide an answer. My uncanny ability to overthink nearly everything, coupled with my neurotically perfectionistic tendencies, speaks to the reason why it has taken me so long to formulate a response. The reality is, as each day passes, I am learning new things about myself and learning to love and embrace those changes through radical acceptance. So my answer to this yesterday, may not be my answer tomorrow and that is okay!

As I evolve, I recognize that the truest version of myself, like all humans, remains the same: we are all innately goo, we deserve love and abundance, and we all have the capacity to improve and do great things.

As I began to list the components that describe me as a human, I concluded that the best way to describe the woman that I am is to simply say, I am an enigma.

Some of the many paradoxical components that I came up with to best describe me are as follows: I am a woman – however, according to the social norms that plague our perceptions, some other qualities I possess are often understood as more masculine (e.g. strong willed, outspoken, tenacious and powerful.)

I have always been inquisitive, as demonstrated by me regularly challenging social norms and questioning all figures of authority with whom I have interacted (sorry for my teenage phase, mom and dad) I am an advocate. I am action-oriented. I speak my mind and I am bold, sometimes even a little crass – however, I believe that I maintain a fair sense of situational awareness and always try to be kind.

I am a daughter, a sister, a granddaughter, a niece, a friend, a dog mom and lover of animals and children.

I am fiercely loyal, but do not trust easily.

I love to be around people who inspire me and contribute positively to my life but need and value my time alone.

I am a leader. I am ambitious, tenacious and incredibly stubborn. I am a risk taker and transparent, yet I struggle with vulnerability.

I am an avid seeker of love, knowledge, fairness and truth.

I make sense of the world and all human experiences through a spiritual (not religious, which to me is an important distinction) lens or an overly intellectual, hyper-academic, rational, and science-based lens. When the two can intersect in my mind, it brings me great joy!

I practice acceptance and love but recognize that I also have a part of me that tends to be extremely critical.

I am intuitive and extremely self-aware, which can be both a curse and a blessing.

I am educated but try to stay humble and have a sense of genuine appreciation for the phrase "the more you know, the less you know."

All in all, I am a woman with many complexities trying my best to accept myself for all that I am each day while living a life full of love and abundance.

What do you do for a living? Why did you choose it?

I am a licensed mental health professional and social entrepreneur. I am the co-owner of The Fearless Kind, offering inpatient rehabilitation for young adult women seeking recovery from a substance abuse disorder. I have a Ph.D. in Marriage and Family Therapy from Texas Tech University in the Community, Family and Addiction Sciences Department.

I often say that the profession chose me, more than I chose the profession. Form a young age, people have always shared with me their secrets, pain, and feelings – whether I was ready to hear it or not. I always knew that I wanted to get my doctorate but thought that I wanted a career in academia. After spending several years in higher education, I realized that working in an institutionalized environment was not a good fit for me. I wanted to make changes in the field, do things differently, and help others in more effective and ethical ways. I knew that making the decision to start my own business was a risk worth taking, as it has allowed me to embrace my power, be of service to others, and challenge myself in new and exciting ways each day. I have been able to incorporate my love for teaching, research, and clinical work into my life as a business-owner.

Why do you think people lack self-love?

I believe people mostly lack self-love because we are rarely taught self-acceptance. We paint a picture in our minds of the way things should be and forget to accept the ways things are. When we are presented with opportunities for growth and expansion, we often want to cling onto the way things were or become too attached to outcomes we have dreamed up in our minds. Especially as women, we are often taught to sacrifice our own needs or change ourselves to make others feel more comfortable. We receive external messages and make sense of them by developing beliefs about ourselves that are contrary to self-love and acceptance.

When we are rejected by a potential partner or when we try on a piece of clothing that doesn't fit, we start to believe that there is something fundamentally wrong with us. If these experiences start at a young age and happen to us enough in our lives, we start to believe that we are not good enough, undeserving and unlovable. We start to only find validation through our external experiences; handing over our power to others to determine whether we are worthy.

I believe that self-love is something we must learn. When we come into the world, we do not get to choose the kind of body we want or the family we receive. Some are born into bodies and families that provide them with far more privilege, resources, and opportunities than others. As adults, we formulate paradigms about the world based on our experiences – both favorable and unfavorable. If we are not taught acceptance and self-love, then we will continue to rely on the perception of others to determine who we are and what our place is in the world. While many are fortuned with the opportunity to break the cycle of unhealthy transgenerational patterns for themselves and generations to come, others may not be a fortunate. Even the opportunity to sit here, on a computer, contemplating and writing about self-love in it of itself is a tremendous privilege I hold and for that I am truly grateful.

When we learn how to love and accept ourselves fully, we are better able to navigate the often-painful external experiences we have and no longer allow such experiences to shape the way in which we see ourselves. We can learn to develop an internal filter for negative experiences in our lives that will allow us to experience pain, learn from the experience, and move forward – not allowing the pain to impact our self-perception, worth and value.

What are you currently working on that is bringing you joy?

Today, I am trying to only focus on the things that bring me true joy. The things in my life that I do to bring me joy now are when I take opportunities to speak my truth and own my power. When I betray myself and act out of alignment with who I am and the things I truly want, it creates a lot of fear and doubt – thus, preventing my ability to experience joy. I have been actively trying to keep my thoughts focused on the things I want, instead of the things I do not want.

I am currently participating in a weekly women's meditation group. It is a place where we all share our joys, struggles, and offer support to one another. It helps me to maintain clarity and focus about the things I want in my life. This group also helps to hold me accountable for the inclusion of daily self-care practices that benefit my mind, body and spirit. I try to stay connected with myself through daily meditation practices and by treating my body well.

Other things that bring me joy are spending time with those I love and who accept me for who I truly am. While I recognize that I am responsible for the way I feel, I also take responsibility for those I choose to allow in my life. When I surround myself with others who are uplifting and who have an ongoing commitment to improving their own lives, I find the time shared with them to be motivating and inspiring, which brings me joy. I also love the work that I get to do each day. While starting my own business has presented many hurdles, it has also taught me a lot about myself and what I am truly capable of accomplishing. Each day, I get to work on creating a company to help serve others in need and use my voice to advocate for those whose voices have gone unheard. The thought of being able to help others brings me great joy.

When you are at peace what are you doing? What does that look like?

My favorite time of the day tends to be in the early morning before the sun comes us. If the weather permits, I like to sit outside in the morning with a cup of coffee and reflect on what I am grateful for in my life. I try to focus on the things I want to accomplish that day and forgive myself for not getting enough done the previous day. It is peaceful just knowing that I can spend time outside each day to reflect on my own life, before most of the population wakes up and before the emails, texts and phone calls start happening.

Other opportunities of peace happen for me when I am building something new. As hobbies, I like to build puzzles, crochet and refinish furniture. When I am doing those things, I can be mindful of what I am doing and I know that the work I put into it will give me feelings of pride and productivity.

What does self-love mean to you?

To me, self-love means staying connected to who I am and what I truly want, without allowing external factors, like the actions or words of others, to influence the way I feel about myself. This has been an ongoing journey for me throughout my whole life. I am grateful for all the lesson that I have learned that have launched me into loving myself more.

I believe that while we are in environments or relationships that provide us with ongoing validation, it is far easier to love ourselves. The real test of self-love is when we are faced with less than favorable or painful experiences that test our capacity to love ourselves. It is not that these experiences will not affect us or cause feelings of sadness, but by always maintaining the internal belief that you are worthy of love and good enough means that you'll be able to navigate those painful external experiences with more ease.

Why do you think self-love is important?

I believe that self-love is important because we must learn how to rely on ourselves for happiness. When we give up our power to things in our environment that we cannot control (e.g., other people), we become dependent upon them to make us happy. Relying on others for our own source of happiness is a vicious cycle that will continually result in disappointment. If you have ever been relied upon for the source of someone else's happiness, you will understand how impossible and exhausting it can be.

When we begin to love ourselves completely, no matter what, we begin to see life through a different lens – thus, we are better able to create a life that we want, instead of trying to create a life we think someone else wants ,which leads to feelings of pain and disappointment. It is easy to love ourselves when the conditions around us are catering to our every need; however, when we begin to accept that we cannot control our environment or those around us, we must learn to seek out the things we need from within. Introspective work and insight fortunes us with the opportunity to regain control in our own lives and appreciate the world around us as it is, instead of how we want it to be.

Do you remember the moment you realized how to love yourself?

I believe that throughout everyone's lives, we are gifted with opportunities to love ourselves fully, even if we have not labeled such experiences as "self-love." I believe that these are the times in our lives when we have been challenged by circumstances or others that may have felt painful in the moment but have actually been beautiful opportunities to better understand ourselves and our own needs. Looking back on my own life, I realize that until now, I would not have labeled these trying times as learning experiences that were teaching me how to love myself. For me, there has not been just one experience to share, but a culmination of times that I have recognized that no matter what, I will be okay. I recognize and appreciate all the challenges that I have overcome, as they have taught me how to love myself more fiercely than ever before. The most obvious examples of self-love lessons that come to mind are associated with my past romantic relationships.

Through each relationship adventure, I have learned how to love myself a little more. In the past, I am beginning to realize that I tend to sacrifice my own well-being and desires to meet the other person where they are at on their journey. I have learned that I do not have to sacrifice my own wants or dim my own light to make others feel more comfortable. When I begin to see that my path is not aligned with that of my current romantic partner's, I initially try harder to get them to join me on my path. After days, weeks, or even months of trying to control the circumstances, I recognize that I am only making myself more miserable. When I learn to accept the other person for where they are at, advocate for my own needs, and finally let go, I feel like I am showing myself the love that I wanted so badly for the other person to fulfill.

When we are in romantic relationships, loving ourselves may become an afterthought when the conditions are going well. The challenges arise when the other person stops behaving in a way that makes us feel happy, which was never their responsibility to begin with! Today, I am learning to stop sacrificing my own wants, routine and desires to make others feel more comfortable while they work through their process. When I can standup for myself within the context of a relationship, I feel like I am taking back my power and giving myself the love in which I deserve. These decisions have not always been easy, but I am so beyond grateful for these opportunities to learn how to love myself more and take back the power in my own life.

What does your support system look like?

I have the most beautiful support system that make my self-love journey much easier than it would be without all their love and kindness. I have beautiful friendships with others that I have created and nurtured over the years. The friends that I have chosen to be a part of my journey are all humans who invest time and energy into improving themselves. Through these friendships, I have laughed, cried, and grown more than I ever imagined possible. My support system also consists of my loving family, who have taught me the value and power of what is means to show up for those you love. I don't even have words to describe the overwhelming amount of gratitude I feel for the support I have in my life.

Tell me about your journey to love.

To me, my journey to love is an ongoing adventure! On my journey, I am learning to accept things about myself that I once believed to be shameful or disappointing. Each day, I try to remind myself that the most important relationship that I will ever have is the one with myself. I am actively trying to find the joy in all the things I do by maintaining a sense of gratitude and self-awareness. When I lose connection with the truest version of myself, I find that I handover my power and adopt the perception that things happen to me, instead of taking personal responsibility for the things that happen in my life. I believe that part of my journey is not to never lose connection with myself, but more about the process of learning to love myself through all my experiences, while being mindful of the gifts that are hidden behind pain and disappointment.

What is your single most embarrassing moment?

I once read a blog post about how to find our life' purpose and one of the steps was to find ways to embarrass yourself. After reading this and continuing to reflect on it over the past two years, I am realizing now that I do not embarrass myself nearly enough. I dispense a significant amount of energy into trying to predict how things will go in my life, while trying to come up with a plan of action for each possible pathway. I am slowly coming to the realization that my efforts are completely futile and that I need to learn to let go more often and embrace the beauty of uncertainty. In relation to self-love, I would say that one of my most embarrassing moments was when I got into a fight my senior year of high school. It was close to graduation and every year my high school did an annual junior class versus senior class powder puff football game. The previous year, I played in the football game and had a great time with my friends! The next year, I was so wrapped up in my dysfunctional and dramatic teenage relationship that I couldn't focus on anything else but that. I knew that my boyfriend at the time was cheating on me with another girl but didn't understand how to love myself enough to leave the relationship and move on to things that were better for me. I remember walking into the powder puff game that year to get my yearbook, watch the game, and see my friends. When I was walking into the game, I remember seeing my boyfriend at the time standing in front of his other love interest, while she was playfully zipping and unzipping his hooded sweatshirt. During my adolescent years, not only was self-love a foreign concept, but self-control and emotional regulation were two things I had yet to discover. After seeing the two of them together, my body was fueled with feeling of hurt and I let anger take control of my body. Without saying a word, I walked right up to my boyfriend, hit him with my yearbook and then turned to the girl and attacked. Where I learned how to fight like that in the moment was beyond me. Afterwards, I remember being pulled off her by my boyfriend and a few of his friends. My friends, and everyone else at the football game, saw what has happened and immediately got me out of the game. After breaking up with him and wallowing in self-pity all weekend, I walked into school on Monday morning hoping that everyone would have forgotten about the incident. As I walked into AP Psychology that morning, my teacher stood up and started clapping his hands and cheering, "Rocky! Rocky! Rocky!" I remember my body feeling flooded with embarrassment. Then he said, "Schonian, next time you fight, let me know so I can put money on it!" I was so embarrassed. I was less embarrassed about the actual fight and more embarrassed about how long I stayed in such an unhealthy relationship. I sacrificed the things that were important to me to devote all my time, energy, and resources toward trying to get some lame high school boy to like me. He was the first boyfriend I ever had, and I allowed him to define my worth by how much he liked and how loyal he was to me. I am lucky that I did not get into serious trouble for fighting at school. I now realize that the only reason I didn't get in trouble was because the teachers who witnessed my moment of destruction saw something in that I couldn't see at the time. I believe now they saw me standup for myself, they saw me take back my power (in a terrible way), and they saw me as someone worthy of a great future full of wonderful things. At the end of class, my psychology teacher asked how I was then he said, "of course you're sad, you're experiencing a loss. Loss hurts, but you deserve better than that." What he said to me that day provided me with a shimmer of hope, when all I could feel was my pain and while I was clinging to the belief that was not worth enough of a loving relationship. While that incident for me was nothing short of embarrassing, I began to recognize that the only reason for me to be embarrassed was because of my reaction to a circumstance in which I had no control. I now understand that the downfall of my relationship was not because I was not good enough or unworthy of love, but because him and I were on two different pathways. I am grateful for the end of that relationship, as well as all the others that have guided me to where I am today. Had any of those relationships in the past worked out, I can with absolute certainty that I would not be the woman I am today. Oh, and for all you readers out there, anger is no longer an emotion that I allow to hijack my feelings. While I appreciate all the things that anger has gotten me through in the past, I haven't experienced reactive anger like that in almost a decade. I also have developed a great appreciation for the Hulk, specifically when Bruce Banner says, "you wouldn't like me when I'm agry." I get it Bruce, I really get it.

How do you embrace your self-perceived flaws?

I am learning to embrace my self-perceived flaws each day, including the times I allowed myself to Hulk when I felt hurt. I have learned to embrace my own flaws each day by learning to accept the things about myself that I cannot change, including anything and everything that I have said, done or felt in the past. There isn't anything I can do about what happened yesterday, all I can do is focus on today and where I want to be tomorrow.

I am also working on accepting parts of myself that may be challenging for others to accept. Part of my self-love journey is to remember that I do not have to dim my own light for others to feel good about themselves. I am working on this by owning my own power and continuing to speak my truth, no matter what.

You are going to dinner…where do you go and what do you eat?

This is a great question. Part of my self-love journey is trying to remember to nurture my body with healthy and energizing foods, while balancing my occasional desires for overindulgence (e.g., eat all the bread things). To keep it relatively general, I would try to select a locally owned business, because I like to support small businesses, and a place that has great bread, ambiance, meal options without meat (that aren't just salad), and a diverse range of dessert selections (just in case).

Do you believe a higher power is at work in your life? What impact does that have?

Yes, absolutely. While I am not a religious person, I do identify as spiritual. I whole heartedly believe in the power of energy created through our thoughts, actions, and emotions. I believe that the energy we carry around with us contributes to the paths we choose and the way in which others respond to us. My belief in something more powerful than myself provides me with a sense of inner peace and an increased awareness of how I can only control myself, not anything or anyone else.

I used to think it was cliché and ridiculous when people would say things like "well it just wasn't meant to be" or anything closely related, but now I have begun to realize the validity of those statements. While those things are hard to hear in moments of pain, as I continue to work on my spiritual self, I have developed a richer understanding and appreciation for why letting go of the things that no longer serve me is of utmost importance. Letting go of the perceived notion that I can influence the choices, beliefs, and emotions of others has been a profound learning experience for me. While I do believe that we have freewill, I also recognize that the Universe or energetic field around us give us exactly what we need, when we need it. When we miss those opportunities for self-reflection and growth, I believe that we are given another similar experience to learn from again.

I do not believe that these gifts we receive from the Universe in which we are a part of are malicious or dogmatic in any way. I believe that these gifts are opportunities for us to love ourselves and one another more than we could ever imagine. We live in a beautiful world, full of beautiful people and it changes each day. When I challenge myself to pay attention to the beauty that surrounds me and appreciate the world as it is, my capacity for unconditional self-love and the love I give others expands – thus, making any painful experiences far more manageable than ever before.

What is your number one piece of advice for women learning to love themselves?

Do not wait for anyone or anything to tell you how you feel, who are you are, which decision to make, or what/who you like. You are perfect just the way you are, and you should never let anyone else determine your value.

Develop a close, personal relationship with yourself and pay attention to how YOU feel in every room you walk in to, around every person you meet both new and old, and trust the way that you feel. Make decisions based on how you feel. Listen to the little voice inside your head, trust your gut, and GO FOR IT. If people don't like it or if they don't like you – screw 'em, because why on earth would you want someone who doesn't like you anyway?

How can women connect with you?

Email: sschonian@fearlesskind.com
www.fearlesskind.com
www.fearlesskind.org
Instagram : @drosarahscho
@thefearlesskind
@recovereverything

Closing

This is a full on commitment. As Kelly Cutrone – my mindfulness goddess – said, I hope that you too will have a journey, instead of just a life. Actually, I hope it's a full-on expedition.

I want you to choose to live your expedition. Allowing others on the ride with you. Teaching people the concepts you have learned to change your life.

Made in the USA
Monee, IL
04 February 2020